PRAISE

"*Psychedelics, Transcendence and Spirituality*, by Winston Hampton, is a must read for any spiritual aspirant, psychological therapist, spiritual advisor, health practitioner or social planner who truly wants to understand the impact of psychotropic substances on consciousness. His unique journey transformed his deep involvement with psychotropic use and the potential illusions of that world into a comprehensive understanding of its spiritual and psychological impact on human consciousness and its transformation into genuine states of clarity, wellbeing and purpose. This is not a for or against approach. Rather a truthful and comprehension exploration of the impact of psychotropic drugs on our potential for life, health and enlightenment. He is a valued voice in the current dialogue as to the place of psychotropics in our society."
Dr. Robert Waterman, EdD.

"Wow! Your book is amazing. I waded in curious about how your research would help me to develop a better vocabulary and understanding of the relationship between the use of psychedelics and how my psychotherapy clients view their progress towards personal transformation. Your research and writing delivered much more than just a context for understanding the role of psychedelics, but also a greater understanding of assisting clients in obtaining mental tools to increase the sustainability of the experience and the continuance of expanding awareness."
Alexis Saint, M.Ed., LPC-S

"This book is a very important read for our times. As our culture embraces marijuana this book offers some important insights as to the possible impacts. Win's perspective is an invaluable read in terms of considering psychotropics in our present world. Win's approach is a thoughtful, honest and vulnerable. Thank you for addressing this important topic."
Karey Thorne, M.A. LPCC

"If you read but one book on spirituality this year, gift your soul by making Psychedelics, Transcendence and Spirituality that book. A luminous and enlightening book grounded in the author's experiential breadth and depth with psychedelics which transcends the notion that the phenomenology of psychedelic use is the final destination. This seminal book will expertly guide you on how and why to bridge the gap between psychedelic use as initiator and the numinosity of durational transcendence."
Jon Mcintosh, Teacher and guide of heart-centered transformation and healing, spiritual awakening, and discovery of the Authentic Self. guidanceforhealing.com

"Winston presents an exciting exploration into the field of consciousness by going further than biochemical pronouncements of reality in relationship to healing and awareness of spirit. He bridges the experience of consciousness, the sacred and the divine, into a practical reality that is inherent in everyone. Simply put, we are more than our mind, emotions, and our bodies. We are awareness, a loving knowing of oneself outside of time and ego. We are a harmonious field of energy. Who we are is soul, not an ego-bound body. I highly recommend this work as an enlightening read. Bravo, Win!"
Peter Bailey

"Winston Hampton's book on psychedelic drugs and the human energy system is must-read material for researchers and scientists of consciousness. His deep care and loving caution are personally-informed data, driving an important dialogue at this point in our profession's conversation about drugs, spiritual awakening and sustainable transcendent awareness. Thank you, Winston, for your insightful contribution at this important time."
Karen M. Faherty, Ph.D., Clinical Psychologist, EMDR Certified Therapist

"Insights and perspective-shifts abound throughout Psychedelics, Transcendence, and Spirituality. Author Winston Hampton articulates the next frontier of research into psychotropic substances. He urges the use of a Quantum lens to understand the effects of these drugs on the invisible energetic structures of the human anatomy beyond the allopathic-only model. For open-minded scientists, healers, medical professionals, and explorers of consciousness. He offers food for pondering as he shares his personal experiences, study and research, and nuances of embodied wisdom from a lifetime of effective spiritual practices. He illuminates challenging materials and weaves in new perspectives to illustrate how the entirety of the body's multiple energy fields are affected by psychedelics in contrast to experiences of spontaneous spiritual transcendence."

BJ Middendorf, Yin Arising Mentor,
Catalyst for Conscious Creators
www.WriteSynergies.com

"Winston Hampton's book is transformative in the ideology he brings forward towards modern science and the opportunity for all of us to reevaluate our conditioned perspective towards both medicinal research and drugs with hallucinogenic properties. The awareness he brings forward cuts through much of today's modern hype on drugs and the Newtonian perspective and allows for a more expansive perspective on the effects of these new modern-day drugs, such as marijuana. He provides a holistic vantage point towards conventional scientific approach. It is a book for anyone working with or ingesting any type of psychotropic drug".
Edie Willey, MAOP, MACP, MASP, MSS, DSS
MA in Organizational Psychology, MA in Consulting Psychology,
MA Spiritual Psychology

"Your perspective is always limited by how much you know. Expand your knowledge and you will transform your mind."
Bruce H. Lipton, *The Biology of Belief*

PSYCHEDELICS, TRANSCENDENCE AND SPIRITUALITY

PSYCHEDELICS, TRANSCENDENCE and SPIRITUALITY

Winston Hampton, M.A., M.S.S., D.S.S.

AwakenNow Publications

Copyright © 2023 by Winston Hampton

All rights reserved. No part of this book may be reproduced or utilized in any form or by any means, electronic or mechanical, including photocopying, recording, or by any information storage and retrieval system, without permission in writing from the author.

ISBN: 978-0-9992039-8-9

eISBN: 978-0-9992039-9-6

Library of Congress Control Number: 2023903183

The author of this book does not dispense medical advice or prescribe the use of any technique or drug as a form of treatment for physical, emotional, or medical problems without the advice of a physician, either directly or indirectly. The intent of the author is only to offer information of a general nature to help in the quest for emotional and spiritual well- being. In the event you use any of the information in this book for yourself, which is your constitutional right, the author and the publisher assume no responsibility for your actions.

Quotes herein are reprinted here as they appear in their original publications to the best of my ability. Quotes throughout this book include authorship and publication title when the information was available. All quotes are intended to be in context and with full transparency. My intention is to give full acknowledgment to the authors and the publication's copyright rights.

Cover design: David Sand

Editor: Richard Keller

Send any correspondence directly to the author. He is interested in a dialogue that supports our need for a global consciousness shift.

williamhmptn@gmail.com

Also By Winston Hampton, M.A., M.S.S., D.S.S.
Rumi Would Have Laughed: Mystical Love Poetry
Available on Amazon in Paperback and Kindle

Gratitude

First, to my parents who loved and supported me no matter what.

Then to my teachers in Spirit and consciousness who assisted my awakening as a spiritual being. Special thanks to John-Roger, John Morton, Robert Waterman, Ellavivian Power, and Ron & Mary Hulnick.

And to all those brave Souls throughout time who risked life, limb, and reputation to bring forward new awarenesses in the face of tradition, superstition, or popular culture who attempt to quash the new awareness to maintain the status quo.

CONTENTS

Introduction 1
PART I: NEW WAYS OF SEEING 7
   Chapter 1: Quantum Worldview 9
   Chapter 2: Be A Spiritual Scientist 17
PART II: QUANTUM MODEL OF CONSCIOUSNESS 27
   Chapter 3: Your Five Bodies 29
      Multidimensional Us 32
      Singular Energy Field or Antimatter 35
      Authentic Self 36
   Chapter 4: Etheric Template and Chakras 39
      Seven Chakra Centers 41
   Chapter 5: Know Your Three Selves 47
   Chapter 6: Gift of the Subconscious 53
      Holding Field Dynamic 55
      Integrating Field Dynamic 57
      Information Flow Dynamic 58
      Note to the Subconscious 61
   Chapter 7: Cell Level Memory, Ego, Aura 63
      Cell Level Memory 63
      Essential Ego 65
      Auric Field 67
**PART III: DIMENSIONS OF DRUGS AND
CONSCIOUSNESS** 71
   Chapter 8: My Marijuana Experiences 73
      Remember What? 74

    24 and Stuck At 14 76

    I'm Not Motivated 80

Chapter 9: Marijuana Energy Field Effects 83

    Auric Snowstorm 85

    Magnetic Field Disruption 87

    Hallmark of Illusion 89

    Radiant Energy Blocked 89

Chapter 10: Psychedelic Experience 93

Chapter 11: Psychedelic Dynamics 105

Chapter 12: Psychedelic Energy Field Effects 117

    Auric Field Effects 118

    Chakra Opening 123

    Microdosing 127

Chapter 13: Subconscious Help or Hurt 129

    Vital Patterns 130

    Pattern Interruption Pros & Cons 131

    Disruption of Higher Guidance 133

Chapter 14: Plant Spirit Guardians 139

Chapter 15:--Which Drug? 145

    Stimulants 145

    CBD 146

    Tobacco 148

    Alcohol 150

    Prescription Drugs 152

    Pain Relievers 154

PART IV: TRANSCENDENCE 157

Chapter 16: Revelations of Transcendence 159

    What We Call Transcendence 159

Spontaneous Transcendence 162

   Psychotropic Transcendence 168

PART V: HEALING, REGENERATION, AND UPLIFTMENT 173

   Chapter 17: Psychological Approach to Healing 177

   Chapter 18: Energetic Approach to Healing 179

   Chapter 19: Spiritual Approach to Healing 185

      Invocation 187

      Visualization 188

      Chanting 190

      Meditation 192

   Chapter 20: Afterthoughts 197

GLOSSARY 209

BIBLIOGRAPHY 217

About Winston Hampton 223

"The fact that science led me to spiritual insight is appropriate because the latest discoveries in physics and cell research are forging new links between the worlds of Science and Spirit. These realms were split apart in the days of Descartes (and Newton) centuries ago. However, I truly believe that only when Spirit and Science are reunited will we be afforded the means to a better world."

Bruce H. Lipton, *The Biology of Belief*

Introduction

There are three great influences in my life that have shaped what I share here. The first and primary force is my inner drive to explore and know myself, my consciousness, and the universe as fully as possible. This is my focus on spiritual awakening. The second great influence is all the lessons, experiences, and learnings I received doing a series of high-dose psychedelic trips. The third is my intensive training over many years studying who we are as spiritual/energetic beings. Our biological anatomy is our energy anatomy manifest. Our psychological states are felt-sensed experiences of energetic conditions within our energy anatomy.

My curiosity about drugs was prompted first by my innate drive to know myself; Who am I? What is the purpose of life? Why am I here? I was 14 in 1969. The 60s and 70s were a time to break out of old outdated ways of living, a time of exploration and experimentation in America. As a young teen, I was so attracted to the ideas and philosophies at the time: Turn on, tune in, and drop out. In 1969 I smoked my first marijuana joint. Within a year or so, when I was 15, I tried my first psychedelic.

A small group of us had access to relatively pure LSD. We started with high doses of 400 to 500 micrograms (mcg), and within a year I was upping that to around 1000mcg. We began to purposefully plan the set and setting of our trips to support inner exploration. I became a trip guide for others. My personal explorations quickly evolved into earth-shattering mystical experiences. I had profound spiritual realizations that have stayed with me my whole life.

My drug explorations went on for 10 years. Over four of those years I did around fifteen high-dose trips, most of them in a, somewhat, controlled set and setting. The high-dose experiences super-charged my entrance into greater spiritual awareness and ushered me into the life-long pursuit of spiritual awakening. Those high-dose experiences were crucial for me to be able to share what this book is about.

I got involved in other drugs too. During this time, I was constantly experimenting with how a variety of drugs affected me. I became a dedicated pothead for many years. I experimented with all kinds of drugs and eventually found myself dependent on drugs for feelings of well-being.

Around age 23 I hit a wall. My drug days gave me considerable thrills. I had realizations and openings that are hard to describe. But I had to admit to myself that some of the drugs were now running me. I hit a wall of limitations and addiction. It was clearly time to move on.

My deep and abiding search for meaning led to my next steps. I was guided by amazing consciousness teachers who taught me how to cope with my addictions and engage my true self in sustainable ways. I met my spiritual teacher who showed me tried and true ways to clear and clean up my life. I began to find balance. One of the truly great gifts he gave me was to teach me how to have highly potent, profound mystical experiences by doing a spiritual practice. These experiences were and are a continuation and confirmation of experiences I had during my high-dose psychedelic trips.

I settled into a lifestyle that no longer included drugs. On one hand, I was learning ancient spiritual practices from a master teacher. On the other hand, I was in school engaged in a very metaphysical master's level counseling degree. The training included energy medicine or vibrational medicine in the form of aura balancing or Noetic Balancing. (see the glossary for more details).

Noetic balancing is a spiritually oriented healing modality. Noetic places the individual energy field into the presence of a universal field. As practitioners we strive to 'get out of the way' and allow the higher frequencies of Light, the spiritual frequencies to come forward and guide the balancing and healing for the highest good.

A pendulum is used to balance the aura, reveal psychological blocks, and clear them. Awareness of the human energy field is essential to the training. Awareness of higher frequencies of spiritual energies, *radiant energies*, transcending the physical is part of the training. I could already perceive auras. I learned how states of energy show up psychologically. I trained to perceive *energetic structures* in the aura and how to engage the client to bring them to conscious awareness and clear them. The clearing process naturally brings life-lesson realizations.

As my awareness cleared and expanded, I learned a great deal about the invisible effects my drug use had on me. I learned in detail how psychoactive drugs affect the human energy fields. I began a deeper process of healing and balancing in my life that, as time went by, brought me ongoing, sustainable fulfillment. My spiritual eyes were opening.

My spiritual teacher, John-Roger*, whose awareness level was indescribable, showed me many subtle lessons beyond the veil. When I met him, my psychedelic lessons were fresh as well as drug effects in my energy bodies. Since he could fully see auras and the full human energetic spectrum, he taught me about very subtle and mostly invisible effects resulting from my psychotropic drug use.

---

*A nice introduction to John-Roger is found by reading *Soul Transcendants: Stories on the Path Home to GOD*, Stories by his students compiled by Jackie Peterson. John-Roger wrote over 40 books and innumerable articles, created a number of self-growth and service organizations, and gave thousands of lectures, seminars, and workshops which were recorded. He traveled and worked with people in almost every country on the planet. His students are a global community.

I want to share what I've learned. I am sharing information here about psychotropic drug effects you won't find anywhere else. People wonder if using psychedelics to help them in their lives is a good idea. People wonder if marijuana is a support or a block to a more elevated spiritual life. The revelations I share provide a whole new clarity about how psychotropic drugs relate to the spiritual seeker and their journey. This information comes out of the new paradigm, a quantum perspective, a holistic perspective that changes how we do almost everything.

We are at a pivotal time of evolutionary change. The information in this book is from a quantum perspective: we are made of energy. It is crucial to know we are energetic/spiritual beings. As energetic beings, we are fully part of the invisible, intelligent, interconnected Web of Life. Seeing and understanding we are energetic beings living in a wholly interconnected Web of Life is crucial to the transformation of global human consciousness at this time!

Part I introduces a Quantum Worldview. In my meaning here, a quantum lens of perception is more than an awareness of quantum physics. In a quantum view everything is made of energy, the world we see has an underlying foundation which is invisible to the material-oriented eye. Human consciousness takes on a whole new orientation when seen through quantum eyes. Our psychology, our biology, all our experience is deeply enmeshed with the invisible energetic world.

Part II outlines the energetic human being. To truly understand the subtle effects psychotropics have on consciousness, we must expand our understanding of consciousness. Our energy anatomy precedes our biochemical make-up. Much of our biochemical systems and functions are prompted from our energy anatomy. Newtonian science sees much of our biology as the cause for conditions in our consciousness. Actually, activity in our energetic anatomy is the cause and the biology is effect. Newtonian science studies the biological effects with no awareness of the energetic causes. Our awareness of this needs to expand!

In Part III, I share my personal experiences with marijuana and psychedelic use. I outline the dynamics of high-dose experience. Then I explain psychotropic effects on consciousness from a quantum perspective. Quantum effects transcend the Newtonian viewing point. For psychotropics to have any value to our spiritual expansion and for any therapeutic usefulness, the effects taking place energetically must be looked at and included.

Part IV provides revelational information on transcendence that presents a new echelon of understanding. Psychotropic transcendence is wholly different from mystical, natural or spontaneous transcendence.

Part V presents holistic ideas for healing and balancing consciousness.

PART I:
NEW WAYS OF SEEING

"The new shift in thinking is the gateway to human transformation. And because of the sheer number of people involved in this shift, and the growing magnitude of the crises that are driving us to change the way we think, we are standing on the threshold of human transformation at a level unlike anything ever before known on Earth."

Gregg Braden, *AZ Quotes*

Chapter 1:
Quantum Worldview

"What they (scientists; physicists) have discovered is nothing less than astonishing. At our most elemental, we are not a chemical reaction, but an energetic charge. Human beings and all living things are a coalescence of energy in a field of energy connected to every other thing in the world. This pulsating energy field is the central engine of our being and our consciousness, the alpha and the omega of our existence."

Lynn McTaggart, *The Field*

I have learned to see through quantum eyes. I believe we must include our awareness of quantum findings in our approach to all sciences, especially those studying human consciousness, biology, medicine, and psychology. I think that expanding awareness of ourselves as energetic beings is one of the crucial building blocks needed toward creating a true paradigm shift in consciousness. The shift we are moving toward is a new echelon of human consciousness.

A **quantum worldview** acknowledges and sees the interconnectedness of all life. It recognizes that all of the systems making up our world and ourselves are one interconnected ecology. It transcends barriers of separation that allowed us to manipulate our world with unforeseen toxic side effects. A quantum worldview is a truly holistic view revealing all of life as a whole, more than a collection of parts.

The quantum view bridges modern science and spirituality. Quantum science says everything is made of energy. Spiritual teachings say everything is made of energy. Seeing through quantum eyes is a newer and higher order of seeing. Quantum eyes include invisible energy forms and fields that have been neglected, ignored, and overlooked. These invisible fields are the fabric of interconnection underlying the ecology of oneness.

You probably learned about Sir Isaac Newton at some point. Along with Rene Descartes, Newton laid the foundation for modern science in the 17th century. Mathematics was his thing. He saw the world as an equation to solve.

He developed a way of reducing everything he saw and wanted to study to a simple formula (*reductive*). For example, the formula 1+1+1= 3 could be applied to studying the world and make it easier to understand (the mathematical process of 1+1+1=3 is considered *mechanical*.)

He reduced complex problems in the world to linear mathematical formulas, thereby revolutionizing and opening the way for modern science. He founded a new mindset to view the world which we now call Newtonian Science (Newtonianism). This mindset is a whole philosophy. This approach is *reductive* and *mechanical*. Almost all our sciences such as biology, astronomy, anthropology, and psychology are studied and researched using the Newtonian model.

If you have a headache, the Newtonian model seeks a pain killer to dull the pain. The reduced path is pain, finding a solution, and killing the pain. It doesn't notice the nail stuck in the side of your head.

When looking for the source of the headache it cannot see the whole picture, including the invisible interconnections. The Newtonian approach simply cannot include the invisible energetics of the whole picture. Newtonian healthcare is called Allopathic Medicine, which means treating the symptom.

Newtonianism sees the world in a one-dimensional plane. It is not able to include the deeper relationships and complexities of human health, well-being, and consciousness. The reality is that Newtonian science is a dead-ended and closed-ended approach. It only looks at what is physically visible and excludes the multiplicity of invisible connections, the whole surrounding ecology.

Here are a few examples of results or side effects using the closed-ended perspective, there are many:

- In the 1950s and 60s, thalidomide was given to pregnant women for nausea. It was later discovered to cause deformed babies.

- Cigarettes, initially marketed as healthy, were later found to cause cancer.
- PCBs (Polychlorinated Biphenyls), used in electrical, consumer, and industrial products, gave rise to nervous system damage.
- Agent Orange, a defoliant used in the Vietnam War, affected soldiers once they returned home with cancer and other deadly diseases.

There are literally thousands of such examples!

In all cases, full effects were "discovered" later. Modern times are full of stories like this in most sciences, pharmaceuticals, and social/cultural/ethnic experiments. The Newtonian approach repeatedly results in tragedies caused by one-dimensional thinking. Attempts to solve problems caused by seeing the world this way end up creating more complex problems. The mindset that created the problems is not able to resolve them.

Newtonian philosophy says the physical, biological body creates consciousness. Its reliance on the physical form is outdated. It ignores quantum findings, which reveal consciousness as it truly is, in all its multi-faceted, multi-directional interconnectivity.

The complex and rampant issues and crises we face ecologically, politically, medically, and culturally will not be resolved using Newtonian Science. We must raise our mindsets and worldview to a new viewing point.

Quantum physics offers the conclusion that people are made of energy, not just matter. I see quantum scientists moving toward territory long occupied by mystics. Quantum physicists and mystics agree on many things. They talk about it in different ways. Quantum physics demonstrates phenomena that are impossible according to Newtonian science. The oneness of all things is possible as a quantum principle and is a mystical experience.

Holograms model the whole and each of its parts as the same. Holograms are based on String Theory, which is based on quantum science. String theory says the universe is made of energetic strings rather than particles. The strings are vibrational loops, each with its own characteristic frequency. In the world of energetic strings, any part contains the whole. In consciousness, each human as an individual particle contains the whole.

Dr. Richard Gerber, author of *Vibrational Medicine* says, *"The hologram provides us with a new and unique model which may help science to understand the energetic structure of the universe as well as the multidimensional nature of human beings."*

Humans are spiritual beings made of energy. Changes to any part of me affect all of me. If I chop my finger, it's not just one linear cause- physical damage, with one linear effect- physical pain. It could also cause emotional and mental trauma, possibly resulting in Post Traumatic Stress Disorder (PTSD). The quantum view sees multi-directional cause and effect in all directions, not just one linear line. This is a holistic lens.

Gerber also says, *"One of the prime differences between the approaches of Newtonian and Einsteinian medicine is their viewpoint of the human body. Newtonian mechanistic thinkers, albeit sophisticated in the molecular biological approach, see the human body as a series of intricate chemical systems powering a structure of nerve and muscle, flesh and bone. The physical body is viewed as a supreme mechanism, an intricate physical clockwork down to the very cellular structure."*

Yet, the consciousness of a human being is so much more than an intricate biochemical system. We are so much more than biochemistry. In fact, our biochemistry is often the effect caused by our energetic selves and the energy fields of our interconnectedness. We are multidimensional beings deeply connected with the universe on multi-levels. We exist in a web of life, wholly interconnected with others and our universe.

I'm not denying the progress western medicine has made to repair our bodies. There is a mastery of physical body repair. Medicines have greatly increased longevity and disease resilience. Yet, these technological strides take place amidst a large number of side effects and mistaken tragedies.

We have prescription drugs for many diseases, psychological and biological. We've established a culture of suppression. No one seems to notice how Newtonianism promotes the suppression of our feelings while ignoring our deep connection to life around us. For instance, it's normal to take prescription drugs with life-threatening side effects. We are amid an opioid epidemic. Depression, stress, and anxiety are nicely suppressed but not comprehensively cured by drugs. We find ourselves calling out for so much more than a quick fix.

The unforeseen side effects that come with reductionist, mechanistic ways of thinking become whole new strings of problems. Overall, our intentions are good. We do want to heal, cure, and make life better. The issue is the mindset or worldview. Newtonian Science is dead-ended because the approach itself does not lead us to fulfillment, joy, and loving, which are necessary for the true quality of life.

We must open up to new ways of seeing! To view the world through quantum eyes is to be inclusive. Acknowledge and embrace the connectivity between us and the world before we destroy ourselves. Quantum seeing is a paradigm shift away from the endless issues caused by seeing humans as machines and reducing them to a mathematical formula. Realizing our oneness and connectivity moves us into deeper caring and fulfillment with ourselves and others.

The quantum lens becomes a dramatically different way of seeing the world in my experience. It is an expanded view of our reality. I honestly don't know how the study of all the sciences will work if we include the energetics underlying all things. But I trust that universal intelligence will guide and support us in discovering this.

As we move into connectivity, multidimensionality, and oneness of all things we meet the **highest good**. As we intend, pray, or request something from life or a higher power, we include "for the highest good of all concerned." This is in direct alignment with the pervasive higher intelligence of the universal field of Being.

Embracing the highest good naturally releases control. In this way, we acknowledge and align with universal intelligence, Spirit, or Source. Many holistic healing and spiritual practices include the highest good in healing work and our movement on a spiritual path.

Chapter 2:

Be A Spiritual Scientist

"Western science is approaching a paradigm shift of unprecedented proportions, one that will change our concepts of reality and of human nature, bridge the gap between ancient wisdom and modern science, and reconcile the differences between Eastern spirituality and Western pragmatism."

Stanislav Grof, *Beyond the Brain*

One of the reasons we take drugs is to see and experience life in new ways. Its seeming purpose is to stretch us into greater spiritual meaning. It's true, new ways of seeing are critically important. We want new ways of seeing that are sustainable. To reach new places inside of ourselves we need transformation to take place. We want a change that stays changed.

A slight shift in our perspective totally changes the world around us. Like when you learn your best friend didn't call you for two days because they lost their phone rather than snubbing you. Different perspectives can really change your reality. I call the way we see our life the **lens of perception.**

Our lens of perception is formed by our gender identity, our cultural values, our education, our experiences, and our beliefs about life. Your birth and the way you are brought up build on this lens. Religious beliefs and schooling play a role. The ego believes the way it sees things is its true identity. However, the lens of perception is simply window glass. Your true identity is the one looking through the window. Spiritual Psychology calls this the **Authentic Self***. Authentic Self is our core self, ultimately our spiritual self.

My electrifying drug experiences gave me knowledge and Reference Points that dramatically changed my life. Further, there are other teachings I learned that have changed my lens of perception just as much or more.

We hope our use of psychotropic drugs acts as an agent to open us to much-needed, uplifting change and expansion, both personally and culturally. Here is an approach I found to be profound, creating a new way of seeing and supporting our wish for greater spiritual connectedness inside ourselves. You must work it for it to work.

Here is the approach of a Spiritual Scientist. It's the ancient spiritual art of waking up to yourself and seeing life more clearly, translated to modern times.

It starts with self-inquiry and proceeds to a plan for transformation. It's a way to direct yourself to find, by direct

---

***Find information about new words and concepts in the glossary.**

experience, what works or doesn't work for you to succeed and be fulfilled on multi-levels. Having direct experience brings understanding, which brings knowing.

Spiritual science builds on self-empowerment. It aligns with the idea that we have inner resources to direct ourselves in our lives. It is an approach supporting the idea that we are already whole, we don't need something outside ourselves to be whole. It is deeply empowering to have purpose and to set out a course of action to fulfill ourselves.

As spiritual scientists, we use our personal experiences to self-direct in finding practical methods to change our lives in positive ways. Here is an example of how I practiced being a spiritual scientist during an intense negative time in my life and brought transformation.

Let's take a trip down memory lane. The infamous economic meltdown of 2007-2009 became a watershed moment. Life had been smooth sailing. However, before I could blink, the real estate market and my assets collapsed. I had major real estate projects going on at the time. Soon enough, I stood at ground zero. Since bad things come in threes, my wife opted for divorce at the same time.

I worked tirelessly and burnt the midnight oil to dodge a crippling bankruptcy. I crashed on the outside, and I was feeling terrible on the inside. I was at war with myself, facing depression and debilitating anxiety inside myself. Something had to give. I was dying inside. I felt unmotivated and lost my enthusiasm for life. Positive change needed to come fast before the hole got too deep.

So, I took the lens of perception of a spiritual scientist and began a journey. Although I sat on the edge of a colossal real estate market collapse and eventual divorce, those disasters were beyond my control. Something else needed to change. My attitude! I learned an important key from therapy previously done. Although I can't control the world around me, I can change my attitude about what is going on. I can choose my response.

I took a close look at my thoughts and behavior (self-inquiry). I became aware right away that I had a pervasive habit of worrying, which caused me anxiety. I saw myself negatively programming my thoughts, my work, and my life. As I looked at myself, I became aware that I worried constantly.

My misery pushed me to form a strong intention. Intention is more than just a thought or desire. It's a creative energy field coming from the Authentic Self. As Carlos Castaneda, the author of *The Teachings of Don Juan* about a Yaqui shaman, said, "In the universe, there is an immeasurable, indescribable force which shamans call intent, and absolutely everything that exists in the entire cosmos is attached to intent by a connecting link." My strong intention would guide the change.

I took some time to contemplate what to do. I thought about what I wanted and how I could get there. I created a plan. As a spiritual scientist, I formed a hypothesis for change: If I do the following six activities, then my anxiety and depression will change to authentic gratitude and enthusiasm in my daily experience.

Here are the six activities:

- Being more mindful of my thoughts throughout the day was key. Whenever I found myself in mind-clenching worry, with great resolve I worked to refocus my thoughts and look at the brighter side of things. If I could eliminate worrying, then the anxiety would go away. As you may know, this was no easy task and required strong motivation.

- I set aside around 45 minutes each morning to read, journal, and contemplate. I made them a priority that came first above everything else.

- I picked two life-changing books: *Spiritual Warrior* by John-Roger and *The Power of Now* by Eckhart Tolle. I read these each morning for about 30 minutes. I planned how I could apply *Spiritual Warrior's* tips and teachings to my life. Meanwhile, *The Power of Now* helped me practice being present here and now to avoid worrying about the future. If I could read and live the advice from these books, then I could actively change my life.

- On top of reading each morning, I journaled anything I felt or thought. I didn't edit my writing at all and let it flow without judgment. If I could dispose of my thoughts on a piece of paper, then I could let go of all kinds of garbage.

- I would find two reasons to be thankful and write them in the journal. If I could come to feel authentic gratitude, then my negative, pessimistic mindset would dissolve.

- Finally, I sat down and did a daily one-hour meditation. I knew how to meditate but I wasn't doing it. If I could cultivate and connect with my spiritual being, I could practice detachment, be relaxed, and rekindle spiritual experiences of enthusiasm, joy, and peace.

It wasn't an easy road, to be honest. I was tangled up in my mental reactive process, so I had a lot of ground to cover. Although I tried to be thankful for something, nothing came to mind. I was desperate at this point, so I decided to fake it until I make it. I learned what I focused on is what I get. I knew the doing of it was key.

Little by little, changes started to happen inside me. I felt them after three weeks of consistent work. Each day I recorded how I felt in my journal to track my progress. By the sixth week, I didn't need to make up a thank you. I began to feel real gratitude for things.

Life started to look up as my attitude shifted. It took me four months to emerge as a happy man from a pit of despair and crippling anxiety. Those lessons are still with me today. The process of using intention along with creating and doing a plan resulted in a transformation inside me.

Later, I realized I had built powerful resilience and inner strength. How interesting! My inner spiritual scientist led the way, building strength all the time. My approach was profoundly self-empowering!

There is a clear, step-by-step system to being a spiritual scientist. It's the same methodology hard science research follows. However, spiritual scientists research themselves. They don't study something in the world. Instead, they observe and direct themselves to discover what does and doesn't work in their direct experience of life.

A spiritual scientist uses this sequential method:

- Start with an intention toward something you want to change in yourself, such as an attitude or behavior. Intention guides the process.
- Ask yourself questions and more questions.
- Observe what is already present and write notes for reference.
- Form a hypothesis for the change: If I ... then I will ...
- Develop a method or actions to test the hypothesis.
- Perform the actions for at least 32 days (the time it takes for a psychological change to stay changed)
- Keep written track often of the actions and any results you observe.
- Evaluate, refine, and repeat toward creating what you wish.

I intended to replace my anxiety with authentic experiences of gratitude and enthusiasm. My hypothesis: If I practice mindfulness, read and follow two books, journal unconditionally, write two gratitudes, and meditate an hour each day for at least 32 days, then enthusiasm and gratitude will replace my experience of anxiety and depression.

This is a practical and powerful approach to initiating change and transformation. It is a direct and natural way to find out what works and what doesn't work specifically for you. This is not a mental exercise. Practicing spiritual science is based on performing actions and then watching for changes. In my case, I used it to transition out of mild depression and episodic anxiety. It worked for me this time and other times I have done this.

I found I could use this approach to move into transcendental experiences. Rather than hoping some religious or spiritual methodology would work, I tested each out to find what actually worked. Yes, this does require dedication and fine-tuned awareness over time.

A spiritual scientist uses the "keep it simple, stupid" (KISS) strategy to expand health at all levels and awaken spiritually. Finding what works for you is built on gradual changes and experiences. It's super helpful to note the results of what you try. Use a journal, an app, or whatever you wish to track your results. Make note of your behaviors, actions, consciousness, feelings, and thoughts. You may be surprised at the changes over time.

I use the spiritual scientist lens to make lifestyle changes. I clear bad habits, addictions, and counterproductive behaviors. I also use this to open high-frequency mystical experiences with myself. Being a spiritual scientist is amazingly self-empowering. As I practiced it, I found greater direction and purpose in my life. I became more accountable and did away with the victim card. I found new levels of purposefulness. I now use it as a tool to accomplish wishes, goals, and visions as well as bring sustainable change to my life.

Transformation and sustainable change are crucial as we discover, explore, and follow our spiritual path. Time-honored spiritual practices all align with transformation as a key to our awakening and movement upward.

An *effective* spiritual practice fosters transformation. Ritual and ceremony are more than rote, they are activities that we engage in to access and produce greater loving, joy and inspiration as a living experience.

PART II:
QUANTUM MODEL OF CONSCIOUSNESS

"... the flow of information in a quantum universe is holistic. Cellular constituents are woven into a complex web of crosstalk, feedback, and feedforward communication loops ... To adjust the chemistry of this complicated interactive system requires a lot more understanding than just adjusting one of the information pathway's components with a drug."

Bruce Lipton, *Biology of Belief*

Chapter 3:
Your Five Bodies

"We are beings in dynamic equilibrium with a universe of energy and light of many different frequencies and forms. We are composed of the stuff of the universe, which, as we have already discovered, is actually frozen light. Mystics throughout the ages have referred to us as beings of light."

Richard Gerber M. D., *Vibrational Medicine*

If you want to find the secrets of the universe, think in terms of energy. Everything, including us, is comprised of energy according to quantum science.

As we step into heightened states of awareness, we naturally become aware of our power, existence, energies, and capabilities. Just as modern science dragged us out of the Dark Ages, the emerging holistic worldview will help solve the dilemma of cause and effect.

I became aware of the holistic quantum model of consciousness through a lifetime of research and experience. Knowing an energetic model of consciousness is necessary for a whole understanding of the effects psychotropic drugs have in the energy field of consciousness.

Western culture has made huge advances in the physical sciences. We are masterful at studying and manipulating sciences such as biology or chemistry. We view and comprehend the stars and oceans. We create amazing technology like computers, airplanes, television, cell phones, and robotics.

Newtonian science laid the groundwork for these advances and gives us a beautifully detailed map of our physical bodies. Modern psychology has identified parts of our consciousness. A great limitation is in believing human consciousness is formed and driven by our biological body.

The following chapters present an energetic (spiritual) model of human consciousness. A holistic model recognizes biological parts and then adds energetic dimensions of understanding. Spiritual Psychology recognizes our energy anatomy.

Let's start with our bodies. A Quantum Model of Consciousness includes a basic set of five bodies. Modern psychology identifies these same five as aspects of consciousness and then anchors them to the physical body. Seen energetically, these five are bodies, four of which transcend the physical level. The physical body is the densest of the five.

These five bodies are an ordinary part of our everyday lives. My physical body is the home base for my life. Taking care of my physical body primarily involves rest, eating, hydration, and exercise. I have an imagination. I know I have emotions because I recognize my feelings. I am aware of my mind and thoughts. Plus, I know about my unconscious from my dreams and what psychology has taught me.

The five bodies of the quantum model are:

- Physical Body
- Astral Body (imagination)
- Causal Body (emotions)
- Mental Body (human mind)
- Etheric Body (unconscious)

In eastern traditions, these bodies are also called sheaths because they encase the Authentic Self, the true self. Some Eastern philosophies see the physical body as a vehicle. The five bodies are vehicles and organs of perception. Robert Waterman, EdD said, *"The physical body is an epicenter of experience. Our bodies are the densest membrane of our Soul."*

From our center of awareness as Authentic Self we have our experiences of imagination, emotion, and mind. We observe our inability to have awareness in the unconscious.

Your combined physical senses are a coordinated faculty of perception allowing you to perceive and operate on the physical dimension. Thus, the physical body is an organ of perception for the physical realm. It is the same for each body. Each body is an organ of perception in its respective realm.

Multidimensional Us

We are truly multidimensional beings able to perceive more than one plane of existence at a time. We can be aware of physical pain and strong emotions while thinking a whole train of thoughts simultaneously. Our multidimensional nature is perfectly ordinary.

Now let's add another piece to the five-body model. Seen spiritually or clairvoyantly, we have multiple bodies allowing us to live in more than one dimension at a time.

Our physical body, as a coordinated faculty of perception, allows us to move through the world and be aware of where we are and what surrounds us. We see the sky, hear traffic noise, smell barbecue, and feel our partner holding our hand as we walk. We know the physical dimension best. It's home base.

Each of our bodies exists within a dimension and reality. Just as our physical body exists in the physical realm, each body exists in a realm. The realm of our imagination is the Astral Realm, which is very similar to the physical realm. The vibrational frequencies are extremely close.

The realm of our emotions is the Causal Realm. Here, the way you see and hear is through your feelings. It is called the Casual Realm because, universally, it is a source of causation in the universe.

The Mental Realm is one of thoughts. Perception and activity take place through the mental faculty.

Each realm has its own landscape and attributes playing a part in the formation of a human being. The bodies and realms all have their roles in human spiritual experience and awakening.

Yep, that's right. As human beings, we live in five realms at the same time. We perceive the Astral through our imagination. We perceive the Causal with our emotional body, Mental Realm with our mental body, and Etheric Realm with our unconscious body. These bodies are much more than aspects of physical body consciousness. They do not originate in biological processes. Each energetic body is separate yet wholly integrated into human consciousness.

They vibrate at unique vibrational frequencies. Therefore, all can exist simultaneously in the same space. Each body's rate of vibration matches the frequency of the realm. If you attune your awareness to the vibrational frequency of one of these bodies, then you become aware of that realm. In a sense, this is what psychics and clairvoyants do, although it's a bit more complex than that. This is why these realms are also known as the psychic realms.

Psychic or clairvoyant perception looks through the invisible bodies – astral, causal, mental, or etheric – using the chakra system, a part of our energetic sensory organ system. Psychics or clairvoyants can see, more or less, subtle bodies normally invisible.

Those on psychedelic drugs often find themselves looking into one or more of these various dimensions.

The Etheric Realm is the unconscious aspect of human consciousness. Carl Jung* proposed the concept that we are all connected through the collective unconscious, and within the unconscious are archetypes. Archetypes are energetic seed forms in consciousness. In mystical literature, the etheric realm acts as a guardian to the gate of spiritual transcendence.

The five bodies and realms, our physical, imaginal, emotional, mental, and unconscious aspects are based on magnetic polarity. Magnetic polarity has a positive and negative pole. There is a magnetic energy field formed between the two poles. Creation, all universes, solar systems, our bodies, and the five realms manifest within this bipolar magnetic field. The physical laws of our universe are based on this bipolar field.

You can grasp the reality of this bipolar magnetic field we live in by observing how the world is made up of opposites. For example, yin/yang, up/down, hot/cold, male/female, empty/full, fast/slow, etc. All things in the material/psychic worlds have a beginning and an end.

Then there is a field of existence not based on a bipolar magnetic field. It is a singular energy field. This field wholly

*Carl Jung (1875-1961) was a Swiss psychiatrist and psychoanalyst who developed psychological concepts such as synchronicity, archetypes, and the collective unconscious.

transcends and is above and beyond, the psychic/material worlds.

Singular Energy Field or Antimatter

From a quantum or spiritual perspective, there is a living intelligence field within and underlying all things. Some names for it are Higher Power, Original Source, or Spirit. This is the immeasurable, omniscient, and infinite original source field within which all things exist. The original source is a singular energy field transcending duality. Scientists postulate this singular energy as antimatter or dark matter.

Spiritual cosmology helps explain the difference and place for both the bipolar, dual-oriented magnetic energies and the singular energy frequencies, also known as Soul, Spiritual Light, Higher Light, and, in this book, *radiant energies.*

The creation of the physical universes is based in duality. The polarized field created between positive and negative poles is creation.

Our physical body is based in opposites. Our emotions depend on opposites. Even our mental processes take place only within this field. Consider, how do we know the singular field of being if it transcends sensation, feelings, and thoughts? Remember, we are holographic particles of the original Being. When our awareness has moved from ego-centered to Soul-centered we are in direct experience of original Oneness.

When mystics speak of Oneness, ultimately, they are referring to the infinite intelligent field transcending all opposites. Knowing the difference between magnetic light and realms and spiritual light and realms comes from direct experience and guidance. The deepest, most mystical spiritual paths lead to original source, to the Authentic Self, into experiences beyond positive/negative polarity.

Authentic Self

We know this singular energy field of Oneness by direct experience within ourselves. All mystical and transcendental experiences touch upon some aspect of this field. Authentic Self is a direct individual expression of it. Authentic Self as a holographic particle of this infinite field contains all its qualities and attributes.

Who we are as an Authentic Self or Soul transcends positive/negative. The Soul is the original pure essence and not a polarized energy form. It is *singular energy*, the pure original essence of the Source or Spirit. I have come to know this as loving, the purest of unconditional loving.

Self-realization, also called Soul awareness, is the direct experience of our Authentic Self, not our ego. Coming into awareness of our true self is the goal of many religious and spiritual traditions. It may be experienced impersonally as a vast unknown or more personally as what I have come to know it as – the Beloved.

Our first full experience of Authentic Self is transcendentally profound. It may include unity, all-is-one consciousness, transcendence of time into the eternal now, and expansive inpourings of wisdom.

As I became more aware of *radiant energies* pouring into my consciousness, I began to discern the effects within each of my bodies. As *radiant energies* mediate through my etheric body, I experienced an ancient, atavistic perception of inception. As the high-frequency energies poured through my mental body, I became aware of vast wisdom pools. As spiritual energies washed over my emotional body, I was overcome with bliss and ecstasy.

All these experiences gave me Reference Points to *radiant energies* that are unfathomable, invisible, and beyond human understanding. The limitations of polar-based magnetic energy fields become apparent through direct experience of the singular spiritual energy fields.

As I became able to sustain awareness in these *radiant energy fields*, which does take time and acclimatization, these experiences normalize. We recognize and realize who we are as a spark of love and holographic particles in an infinite universal presence. We find ourselves in the condition of knowing ourselves as the spiritual being we are.

Chapter 4:
Etheric Template and Chakras

"The etheric template is the template for the etheric body, which then forms the grid structure (structured energy field) upon which the physical body grows."

Barbara Brennan, *Hands of Light*

We all know what a template or blueprint is. It details how a structure comes together. From a quantum perspective, everything in the universe has an energetic blueprint. It's an aspect of universal intelligence. It's how strings in quantum string theory know what to become. It's how quarks, atoms, and molecules know how to form into a particular object.

The human body is constructed from an energetic blueprint. Genetic codes are detailed first energetically. It details where bones, muscles, nerves, and organs go. Traditions of esotericism, Eastern medicine, and energy medicine call this blueprint the Etheric Body Double or Etheric Template*.

*The Etheric Template is different than the etheric body previously described.

While Western science hasn't yet perceived this energetic blueprint, psychics and energy medicine experts sometimes can. It is recognized that including the etheric template in our awareness of human consciousness is useful when looking at health and illness. Health imbalances may be addressed energetically resulting in physical healing.

Any detachment between our physical body and the etheric template results in changes in consciousness and may produce physical body imbalances. A detachment could take place during a car accident for example.

Just as the physical body holds organs within it, the etheric template holds energetic organs such as the chakra energy centers. East Indian Nadis and Chinese meridian system energy pathways connect the etheric template to the various invisible energy bodies. They form an interface between the etheric and the physical body. They are part of energy pathway systems corresponding with the nerve plexus, physical organs, and glandular system.

The etheric template with its chakra energy centers is maintained by the *Basic Self*. I'll describe the Basic Self shortly. In Eastern science, the chakras are an integral part of human psychological makeup. Several yogic traditions utilize this concept for exploring, diagnosing, healing, and expanding consciousness.

Seven Chakra Centers

There are seven major recognized chakra centers.
- Root Chakra
- Sacral Chakra
- Navel or Solar Center Chakra
- Heart Chakra
- Throat Chakra
- Brow or Third Eye Chakra
- Crown Chakra

When seen clairvoyantly, these appear as wheels or flowers with a series of petals. The opening and closing of the petals regulate energy flow and transmutation.

Human consciousness is much more complex than the biochemistry, organs, and systems of the physical body. The physical body is only a small portion of the equation of consciousness.

The energetic chakra system has a fully corresponding physical system. Humans are multidimensional. The interconnection and integration of our five bodies allow this. The endocrine system is the physical side of the energetic chakra system. Thus, the function and performance of the chakras relate to the physical body through the endocrine system. Chakras play their part in physical body health through the endocrine system.

The root chakra's physical partner is the ovaries and testes. The sacral chakra functions through the adrenal glands. The solar center chakra governs within the physical through the pancreas.

The heart chakra corresponds to the thymus. The throat chakra relates through the thyroid gland. The brow and crown chakras govern through the pituitary & pineal glands and possibly the hypothalamus.

The functioning of the endocrine system provides insight into the function of the chakra system. The endocrine regulates and directs many biochemical & organ functions and processes toward health. The endocrine is a messenger system. The chakras regulate in similar ways within the subtle bodies and organs. They are involved in the flow and transmutation of energy through membranes as well as between bodies and levels.

As they circulate and transmute energy, they facilitate the usability of multiple energies within the human system. They integrate from emotional to physical, for example. Chakras are crucial to the balance of cohesive consciousness. Since they are essentially portals between the levels, they are also organs of perception.

The development of psychic or clairvoyant ability directly relates to the chakra centers. Dr. Richard Gerber describes it very nicely: *"Each chakra is associated with a different type of psychic function. For instance, the third eye or brow chakra is associated with intuitive insight and clairvoyance. The throat chakra functions during the use of clairaudient skills. The heart chakra has an association with clairsentience and so forth."*

Our subtle bodies and energetic organs, with the physical as our home base, weave the fabric of our consciousness. While Western Psychology has identified emotional and mental activity as fundamental aspects of our well-being, it has not applied quantum science findings to the field of psychology. This would include our energetics.

Our energy anatomy is continuously affected by our experiences. Mental or emotional trauma can cause damage to the fabric or substance of the mental or causal body and chakra organs. One psychological term for this is PTSD. Psychotropic drugs highly impact the subtle bodies and energetic organs.

Knowledge of human energy anatomy adds a paradigm-shifting dimension when working with consciousness. It's like taking off blinders when looking at and working with consciousness. When we add energy anatomy identification to biological identification, our health care process passes over a threshold into a whole new dimension.

Noetic Balancing work is an energy medicine modality. During a session, for example, we approach the throat chakra as the allegorical/energetic location for beliefs and judgments related to expression. We approach the sacral chakra center as the metaphorical anchor point for creative or sexual issues. We work at the feet with issues having to do with our understanding/ misunderstanding or having/lacking a place in the world.

Our human beliefs and judgments manifest as *energetic structures* or *constructs* in our aura. *Energetic constructs* are psycho-dynamic. A disturbance in the sacral center may be related to a belief or self-judgment made in the past related to sexuality or creativity. This may create a disturbance in sexual expression. It may be a judgment related to a past sexual experience. It may be a block related to trauma or disturbance. There may also be an energetic block located in the causal, mental, or etheric body.

These *energetic constructs* lodge in our energy bodies, in our subconscious field, for extended periods of our lives. We recognize some as blocks or challenges in our lifetimes. This could be a fear of heights based on past experience, for example. These blocks become part of our *lens of perception*.

As you see, this approach is quite different than approaching these issues solely biologically. A holistic approach recognizes the influence of energetic dynamics on biological effects. The quantum model is multidirectional. A belief, emotional reaction, or persistent memory is the energetic cause. The energetic causes prompt biological results. Biochemistry now plays a part in the issue.

There is a practical reason why so many people these days use both alternative medicine as well as modern medicine. Using both approaches together is more holistic.

Allopathic psychology approaches the psycho-dynamic presence of an *energetic construct* causing anxiety by suppressing the bio-symptoms chemically. A holistic approach diagnoses the *energetic construct* toward releasing and transforming the actual cause. Transformation is an integral part of the expansion and maturation of consciousness.

Biochemical (drug) support is helpful in the short term and in some circumstances. Yet, in many cases, it becomes suppression which may compound the original issue.

Damage or imbalance to chakras may be caused by trauma or drugs. Forcing chakra centers to open might result in psychological imbalances and, in some situations, severe psychopathologies. I have observed that psychotropic drugs deeply affect the health of the etheric template and its chakra system.

Chapter 5:
Know Your Three Selves

"The idea of the three selves encompasses many explanations for our consciousness. One psychologist said that when we are born, the mind is a tabula rasa (a blank slate). That is right; the conscious mind is blank when we are born. Another said we have racial memory, like a group consciousness or great unconscious. That is right; that is the basic self. Others say that we have total knowledge and awareness. They are also right; that is the high self."

John-Roger, DSS

The **Three Selves** concept is mostly unknown in spiritual traditions, consciousness models, and energy medicine. The Three Selves are the High Self, Conscious Self, and Basic Self.

The **High Self** is our connection to things spiritual. It's the part of us bringing awareness of our spiritual aspect, guiding us from an elevated position. It is our personal link into the invisible spirit realms. It is our built-in spiritual guide. We may experience it as an inner master.

Before we take on corporeal form, our original essence, the Soul, in collaboration with *radiant energy* forms, makes a plan. I call this our **life plan**, but it's also known as a karmic plan or a destiny pattern. The life plan is a rather broad avenue that loosely sets out the necessary ingredients to fulfill the Soul's purpose in life. The High Self's job is to know the plan, be aware of the Curriculum of the Soul, and guide us in our choices in terms of our lifetime spiritual progression.

While the High Self holds this plan for us, it's also a neutral observer and allows the Conscious Self to direct. In other words, the Conscious Self can proceed on-course or off-course. The High Self functions as an elevated guide toward success and fulfillment in terms of karmic fulfillment and spiritual evolution. It is crucial to our path that the High Self guide us even though it may be largely unconscious. One might see the High Self as a guiding angel.

The **Conscious Self** is the center point of awareness entering the physical body from Soul right after birth. It retains awareness of the inner spirit, realms, and destiny pattern. At around seven years old, a memory veil purposefully drops, making inner awareness unconscious for most. The Conscious Self appears as a blank slate or *tabula rasa*. It is educated and shaped by our experiences and physical environment.

In psychology, the principle of Behaviorism primarily relates to the Conscious Self, although a great deal of conditioning also takes place in the Basic Self. It's the part of you reading this book. The

Conscious Self manages the integration of the three selves as well as educating and guiding the Basic Self. We do our worldly activities via Conscious Self.

Practically, we identify the Conscious Self and ego as one awareness. *The Conscious Self rarely, if ever, comes into direct communication with the High Self.* Communication is done via the Basic Self, which provides a connection to the Conscious Self as intuition or inner knowing. A great deal of our inner spiritual guidance comes from the High Self through the Basic Self into our conscious awareness. This line of communication in our consciousness is crucial to health and well-being!

The **Basic Self** is all about the physical and energy bodies. The Basic Self is centered in the belly button area and often operates through the navel chakra. The Basic Self shows up right after conception with the blueprint to build the corporal body. The Basic Self is given the life plan by the High Self and follows directives out of spirit to guide specific activation of the DNA.

Western-based science studies the biology of building the physical body. It has discovered and mapped the DNA genetic code instruction manual. However, it does not know the life plan blueprint and how specific DNA is activated to fulfill the life plan.

Each individual's Soul, High Self, *radiant energy* forms, and Universal intelligence together create the individual life plan. Specific physical characteristics are part of the plan. The DNA needed for the specified physical characteristics is arranged through the parents and their genetic lineage. One of the Basic Self's jobs is to direct the appropriate and specific activation of DNA.

Once the physical body is built, the Basic Self watches over its health and life-support functions, including those at the energetic level. It maintains the etheric template, chakras, and energy bodies. Since the Basic Self's prime directive is to keep you alive, it may resist the Conscious Self's plan to wake up spiritually – to transcend the physical body. During my move away from drugs, I needed to get my Basic Self on board to cooperate with my spiritual progression.

It's very much like a four-year-old. The Basic Self is a rudimentary consciousness in many ways. Yet, it communicates with the High Self, knows and travels the magnetic inner realms, and can time travel. The emotional realm is contained within the Basic Self domain. Feeling is a primary expression of the Basic Self. The Basic Self accesses a great deal of inner wisdom and is helpful to the Conscious Self.

To be in open communication with this aspect of our consciousness is truly helpful. On one hand, we don't want a four-year-old running our life. On the other hand, we can educate, comfort, and treat our Basic Self as a best friend while receiving its wisdom. Some self-growth approaches see the Basic Self as the inner child. The inner child is actually a composite within the subconscious, but relating to it this way works fine.

The Conscious Self must have a clear communication line in relationship with the Basic Self. The Basic Self usually follows the Conscious Self's directives, more or less, or at least we would like it to (this is part of educating our Basic Self).

The Hawaiian Hunas* is one of the few groups aware of the three selves. They found that creativity in the world, or conscious manifestation, is directly related to alignment of the three selves. When the three selves align, a powerfully energetic and creative impulse is generated. This union is an alignment of three levels of consciousness: God source, conscious awareness, and lower self.

We experience this alignment as epiphany, revelation, and transcendence. The alignment gives the Conscious Self access to High Self and Basic Self information. The High Self may transmit, purposefully, through the Basic Self to the Conscious Self, higher Light experiences as ecstasy, or bliss. This may also reflect a direct experience of ourselves as Soul. A close relationship between the three selves supports our spiritual growth and upliftment.

When the three selves communicate and work together, it results in greater health, wealth and happiness, joy, love and

*Hawaiian Huna tradition: the ancient wisdom teachings of Polynesian culture to provide true empowerment to the individual. Based on seven principles: Ike – the world is what you think it is; Kala – no limits, anything is possible; Makia – energy flows where attention goes; Manawa – now is the moment of power; Aloha – love to be happy; Mana – power comes from within; Pono – effectiveness is the measure of truth.

fulfillment. The famed *spiritual marriage* is a union of the three selves. When we are on purpose with our life plan, it results in well-being in our psychological awareness. We experience this as feelings of rightness, on-purposefulness, fulfillment, and assuredness.

Awareness of these three levels of consciousness is extremely helpful. Knowing this helps us as we work with ourselves to clear blocks and addictions, identify psychological disturbance sources, and expand our health, joy, fulfillment, and purpose.

We've all had experiences of being on-course or off-course in the form of intuition. This feeling of rightness becomes a guideline to the *spiritual scientist* inside us, along with demonstrated workability. Blocks can form in our consciousness that interfere with the communication between the three selves in the subconscious area. Our subconscious's healthy functioning is extremely important to psychological health, well-being, and upward movement!

Our awareness of the reality that we have a life plan of purposefulness adds a dimension of security and understanding to our lives. Our quality of experience is often linked to the relationship between these three levels of consciousness along with health and clarity within our subconscious. The use of marijuana and psychedelics has a tremendous impact on the relationship between the three selves.

Chapter 6:

Gift of the Subconscious

"As a man who has devoted his whole life to the most clearheaded science, to the study of matter, I can tell you as a result of my research about atoms this much: There is no matter as such! All matter originates and exists only by virtue of a force, which brings the particles of an atom together. We must assume behind this force the existence of a conscious and intelligent mind. This mind is the matrix of all matter."

Max Planck, *Lecture "Das Wesen der Materie,"* 1944

Just below the awareness threshold of our Conscious Self is our subconscious. In Western psychology, the subconscious is largely a mystery. It acknowledges its presence and has methodologies to work with it but doesn't really understand its function. From a quantum or energetic perspective, we begin to fathom its dynamics.

The subconscious is a field of energy holding all our experiences. It's like a big room where all the different parts of us talk to each other. Below the subconscious is the unconscious. The unconscious is the etheric body and realm. Every human accesses the etheric realm through their etheric body. The etheric realm is a collective repository. Subconscious is part of this.

As an energy field, this aspect of our consciousness exists over, around, and throughout our five bodies and aura. The subconscious is a composite field including all elements of our consciousness, the five bodies, chakra centers, and energetic membranes all contribute to its substance.

The Conscious Self is designed to be in present awareness. As each experience passes and moves to the past, it automatically drops into the subconscious. Some traumatic experiences might drop into this level as quickly as possible to protect our ego. Eventually, all experience goes into the subconscious to be stored, filtered, and transformed.

It is important to understand how the subconscious plays a vital role in psychological health and well-being. Our subconscious must be balanced, vital, and fluid. Many mental illnesses and psychological challenges are associated with blocked and recycling aberrant energy patterns stuck in the subconscious field.

It's nearly impossible to have awareness at the unconscious level. It's designed this way on purpose. The functions of the subconscious act as a golden door. Understanding how it works and working it is a spiritual key. The subconscious also acts as mediator between the unconscious realm and our conscious awareness.

There are several vital functional dynamics that support the transformation of experience into the fabric of consciousness, an integral part of our evolution. There is a **Holding Field, Integrating Field,** and an **Information Flow Dynamic.**

Holding Field Dynamic

Our experiences are fuel for the growth, transformation, and evolution of our consciousness. The subconscious is an important part of the digestion of experience into transformation and wisdom. All experiences drop into the **Holding Field** of the subconscious. The holding function supports a healthy evolution of experience, trauma, and balance in our consciousness. It supports ego health and well-being.

The subconscious field plays an important role in the function of memory. We think of memory as saved playbacks of past experiences. The ramifications of memory are much broader and deeper than this. From a quantum perspective, memory exists in magnetic energy fields both in and outside the physical body as well as biochemical functions in brain tissue. Brain and nerve structures serve as anchor points around which the magnetic fields flow.

As our experiences drop into the subconscious there are multiple levels. A relatively neutral experience is simply stored as a reference point. When we have a *response* or reaction to the experience, then the response is also stored. *Experience and response are two different things.* Responses are primarily emotional and/or mental. Almost all emotional responses are accompanied by a belief or judgment.

Thoughts, beliefs, and judgments have an *energetic structure* or form. This is recognized by many holistic healing approaches.

These *energetic structures* may be perceived clairvoyantly in the human energy field. In Noetic Balancing work we perceive, locate, and access these energetic forms. This is direct access to subconscious material which allows conscious awareness to support transformation. Bringing the material in an energetic construct into conscious awareness is a step to resolution.

In the case of severe trauma, response or reaction may happen instinctually or as a biological morphic field* having to do with survival. It can also be a response of the Basic Self. In all cases, our response in the form of belief or judgment becomes a part of the experience adding to the *energetic construct*. Belief or judgment is what we decided or interpreted about the experience.

The holding pattern is not 'just memory.' Our consciousness is designed to provide movement and transformation of the original response or reaction which remain as active *energetic constructs*. Belief and judgment held in the subconscious field are holographic particles. As such, each *energetic construct* is a link to the whole original experience and to any connected pattern. When we tap into an *energetic construct,* we have access to the whole original experience.

*Morphic Field: The term was coined by biochemist Rupert Sheldrake in the mid 1900s. The presence of an energy field, extending through time and space influencing the organization of coherent systems and patterns, acting as a collective memory guiding cellular development and behavior toward a specific result.

Energetic constructs lodged in our aura or subconscious become part of our lens of perception. For example, if the *energetic construct* holds the judgment that all people with blonde hair are dangerous, when we see someone with blonde hair the judgment is activated, and we *see and feel* them as dangerous. *Energetic constructs* shape our personal reality as a lens of perception we look through and as a lens the universe looks back at us through.

You may ask, why should a judgment about people with blonde hair be something that needs to be completed or resolved? The natural attributes of Authentic Self are loving, caring, joy, and enthusiasm. A belief or judgment that blocks or warps the presence and expression of the Authentic Self calls out for transformation into wisdom to bring greater expansion and vitality.

Integrating Field Dynamic

The holding pattern field has a dynamic within it designed to integrate our experiences in consciousness. It integrates our individual experiences as well as the collective consciousness in the Universal Noetic Field. The **Integrating Field Dynamic** has an energy flow that is a spiral movement.

The spiraling action is designed to purposefully bring held *energetic constructs* to conscious awareness. The dynamic isn't meant to resolve past experiences. Past experiences are simply what they are. Integration is for value judgments or decisions we have formed around our experiences. Resolution takes place as we complete, integrate, and transform a stuck response, belief, or judgment. Stuck responses or reactions call for resolution.

Energetic constructs may surface as memory, anxiety, panic attacks, or as particular imagery in dreams. This is purposeful to complete and transform an experience/response into knowledge and wisdom for our evolution. This is an expansion of awareness or evolving consciousness. This is us finding a resolution for conflicts and challenges from our experience, which builds wisdom. This is us maturing and growing spiritually.

Understanding the purposefulness of the subconscious helps us know how to handle intrusions of subconscious material into waking consciousness. Western psychology already works at finding ways to utilize subconscious material toward resolving issues and greater health. When we know that intrusions serve the purpose of expansion growth and greater fulfillment, we are better equipped to meet intrusions and utilize them for our upliftment.

Information Flow Dynamic

The third vital dynamic within the subconscious is an **Information Flow Dynamic**. The subconscious field is a communication conduit. Communication between the three selves is a crucial psycho-dynamic. I discussed this communication flow in the chapter on the three selves.

While the Conscious Self doesn't have conscious awareness of the Basic Self, there is an essential flow of subliminal information between the Conscious and Basic Self. The Basic Self receives information from the High Self and relays it to the Conscious Self. The communication flow is electromagnetic energy. The flow may be perceived as intuition, inspiration, or a sense of rightness. It could also come across as an invasion of a disruptive subject.

The High Self provides a higher form of guidance. The more guidance we are aware of, the more on-purpose and fulfilled we become. As well as passing guidance along, the Basic Self also assists the Conscious Self with information toward greater health and well-being.

There are two primary ways subconscious dynamics are interfered with or blocked. One is *suppression.* Psychotropic drugs can suppress subconscious dynamics. It may look like a field clogged with static energy, smoke, or dust. This might be energetic drug residue or static energy caused by a polluted mixing of energy frequencies.

If we suppress the natural spiral process of remembering material being brought forward for completion and balance, subconscious memories are more likely to emerge in abrupt, frightening, or disturbing ways. Suppressing the natural process of the subconscious' return of memories can impede natural consciousness evolution.

Some behavior patterns can also block or cause interference in the subconscious field. *Habits, addictions, and obsessions* are powerful energy patterns. Habit patterns start with the Conscious

Self. Habits can start by thinking about something or with a behavior or sensation. Then we add emotion and repetition. A sensation-based habit may include biological dependency with neural pathways built up and reinforced.

Habits and addictions are distinct energy patterns in the subconscious field. Obsessions and addictions may extend into the unconscious and Basic Self. *Obsessive and addictive energy patterns interfere with the communication flow between the Basic and Conscious Self.* As a side note, these obsessive or addictive patterns must be cleared and dissolved to support spiritual growth. Eventually, they block spiritual progression into the Authentic Self.

The Conscious Self gives direction to and educates the Basic Self, which is like a four-year-old but also is in charge of the physical body. The Basic Self relays messages to the Conscious Self from the High Self. When the Conscious Self engages in a habit or addiction, the Basic Self takes this as direction and works to support it. As the Basic relays information, the Conscious Self could mistake the addiction pattern as relayed information. Thus, habits and addictions can be reinforced from both sides.

We also have positive habits. They are energy patterns in the subconscious field as well. Positive habits (such as regular exercise or another daily routine.) generally don't block communication in the subconscious. I mention Pattern Interrupt in Chapter 11 which takes place during during high-dose psychedelic sessions. Psychotropic drugs can interrupt or disrupt any of the habit patterns, positive or negative, in the subconscious field. This could be good news or bad news, depending on what is interrupted.

Note to the Subconscious

One large drawback of the Newtonian view of disturbance and illness through a modern medicine approach is how it sees imbalance. It attempts to heal by simply blocking symptoms biologically as a coping mechanism. This methodology often obstructs awareness of the original cause in the subconscious. It has become common to prescribe psychoactive drugs as a primary treatment method. Painkillers and mood adjusters are examples.

Most, if not all, anxiety, depression, and other psychopathologies relate directly to the subconscious field. Generally speaking, our varying experiences of anxiety and depression are messages from our subconscious. These experiences are brought from the subconscious into conscious awareness purposefully. This phenomenon is 'for us' and is not 'against us'.

The natural dynamics of the subconscious continually work to support our experiences toward resolution and balance for higher evolution. In a sense, you could say, our subconscious gives us an extended period of time to grasp, be accountable to, respond to, transform and integrate experiences into our consciousness to expand our maturity and wisdom.

Optimal ego health relies on a vital and fluidly functioning subconscious. Mood-affecting drugs, like marijuana, end up suppressing these subconscious dynamics, interfering with and blocking *transformation*. The best-case scenario is to suppress the disturbance enough so a person can function somewhat normally. If only for a while.

With the prevalence of side effects, prescribed opioid addiction, and levels of suicide in certain populations, it seems clear the linear Newtonian approach is deeply limited. The holistic quantum worldview is fundamentally different than Newtonianism.

A holistic view recognizes that symptoms such as anxiety or depression are messages being brought out of the subconscious to be utilized toward greater well-being. Yes, suppression is clearly seductive. It can be a quick fix. Yet, in the inner chambers of our heart, what we truly want is transformation of our anxiety, panic attacks, fear and depression.

We want these negative experiences to become fertilizer for healthy buds and flowers of joy, delight and enthusiasm. We want expansion into inner freedom and resilience. And we want these uplifting experiences as expressions of our own inner resources. We want to find our way to a lightness of being that is sustainable.

Chapter 7:
Cell Level Memory, Ego, Aura

"From these energy field observations, you are probably beginning to see the connection between illness and psychological problems more clearly. We stop our feelings by blocking our energy flow. This creates stagnated pools of energy in our systems which when held there long enough lead to disease in the physical body."

Barbara Brennan, *Hands of Light*

Cell Level Memory

Here, **Cell Level Memory** is more than what Newtonian science calls cell-level memory. This includes all physical body cells. Cell Level Memory describes how memories, *energetic constructs,* and energy patterns may contain a cellular anchor point.

As discussed before, each thought, belief, and judgment formed in response to and in conjunction with an experience creates an *energetic form* living in our subconscious and auric field. More than just a memory marker, *energetic constructs* are holographic particles containing the whole original experience.

Our five bodies co-exist vibrating at different frequencies within the same space. A physical experience we have that includes emotion and judgment involves at least three bodies – physical, causal, and mental. Memories or *energetic constructs* of the event may exist in any or all of the three bodies within the subconscious field. Energy patterns such as habits or addictions within the subconscious field are often anchored in the physical body as well.

Energetic constructs, any memory and habit patterns within the subconscious, unconscious, and Basic Self can imprint Cell Level Memory. If the Conscious Self stops indulging in a habit pattern, the Basic Self may still attempt to institute it. Then the Conscious Self educates the Basic Self to release the pattern. When the Conscious Self and Basic Self clear and release the habit, it may still feature a hidden memory marker at the cell level.

Do you know how your computer or an app auto-fills in certain fields? Like in a mail app, it remembers an address associated with a name. Even if you delete the information and replace it in your contact list, the app seems to ignore this and fills in the original information. You need to go deeper to remove previous recipients from the list. This is how Cell Level Memory works.

It's often overlooked as an aspect where energy patterns need clearing and education. Remember, these energy patterns are emotional, mental, or behavioral states. It's especially true with long-term habits and addictions. Patterns don't necessarily clear by simply waiting for the physical body to replace the cells, which it does every eight years or so.

Cell Level Memory most definitely relates to drug dependencies. Even after years of being sober, memories kick in and push a person back into use. Therefore, it could be helpful to be aware of Cell-Level Memory when treating addictions and conditions like PTSD.

There are ways to clear Cell Level Memories sooner than waiting for natural cell replacements. Surgery, clear intention or the presence of *radiant energies* may do it. Some energy medicine practitioners know of cell-level memory and are trained to clear patterns stuck at the cellular level.

Essential Ego

Definitions of ego describe the self that feels, acts, or thinks. It's part of the mind that mediates between conscious and unconscious and is responsible for reality testing and a sense of personal identity. The ego is primarily the interaction of the mind and emotions. From a spiritual perspective, it's an essential pretend self that ultimately serves our awakening as divine beings.

When you mix imagination, emotion, mind, and unconscious with the physical body as the focal point, you need an awareness unifying and correlating all these intersecting frequencies. The ego identifies itself as a physical body with imagination, feelings, and thoughts. Since the physical body is a vehicle and is not our

Authentic Self, the ego is a facsimile self. Eastern spiritual teachings call it the false self.

A healthy ego is imperative to consciousness expansion and spiritual growth. We need a healthy functioning ego to navigate this world. If ego is dysfunctional, this must be resolved so conscious spiritual progression can take place. On the flip side, it might be that a dysfunction was designed for you to come to a resolution to expand in wisdom and evolve.

Ego sees its thoughts and belief systems as essential parts of its self-identity. Ego will defend its beliefs to its death. It goes to great lengths to convince others its beliefs are the true, right way. Ego attachment to beliefs, feelings, and past experiences, in a world where these are constantly changing, creates a psychology that is brittle, crystalized, and ripe for psychopathologies to germinate and grow.

Dysfunction of the ego structure may come from damage in any of the bodies or energy systems. For example, it might be organic damage to the brain, dissociative damage to the mental body, or obsessive damage in the causal body. It's challenging to progress on your spiritual path when you are psychotic, schizophrenic, or suffer a condition like obsessive-compulsive disorder (OCD) even if these experiences are part of your life plan.

Traditional psychology focuses on healing and balancing fractures and imbalances in the ego structure. Spiritual Psychology, as a holistic approach, reframes this into a conscious work of becoming more aware of ourselves as Authentic Self. When our lens of perception includes the Authentic Self, healing and balancing the ego structure takes place naturally.

As spiritual beings moving through life getting experience, ego plays a crucial role. The limited awareness of the ego generates constant experiences that are fuel for our evolution. Eventually, we learn to purposefully move from an ego-centered existence toward a Soul-centered way of life. An *effective* spiritual practice enhances this movement.

Auric Field

The aura is an electromagnetic energy field surrounding and interpenetrating the physical body and is seen psychically or clairvoyantly. Aura has layers and levels to it. It is seen as an egg-shaped energy ball containing a nested hierarchy. Aura has vortices and energy pathways. The aura is a distinct field that is consciousness. All humans radiate this living, moving, noetic energy field ecologically nested within the Universal Noetic Field.

Organs, such as the brain, heart, lungs, and liver emit magnetic frequencies and have their counterparts in our energy bodies. Just as the physical body has dynamic systems moving and interacting as vascular, neurological, lymphatic, and biochemical, the aura has interlacing systems and dynamics such as the meridian system, the Nadis, chakra energy dynamics, and spiraling of the subconscious field.

The aura is in constant flux and movement. Attitudes, endeavors. and state of spiritual connection is portrayed in the colors, vibrations, and formation of the aura. Thought and beliefs with accompanying emotions are holographically stored in the aura as *energetic constructs*. Emotional mental balance and attunement with the Divine support a balanced aura.

The physical body is an extension of the aura. The energy vibration slows until it congeals into form. Thought, feeling, and archetypal energies precipitate into the physical body. This is the Mind-Body connection. The relationship of energetics to biology is multi-directional. Energetics influence biology and biology influences energetics. This is reflected in the auric field.

The aura is a transparent source of information disclosing states of consciousness. That is, qualities of the consciousness are seen for what they are. Dishonesty is seen as dishonesty. Attempts to hide something are seen as an attempt to hide something. Attitudes and belief systems are disclosed for what they truly are in the auric field.

The aura is a beautiful medium for transformation. *Energetic constructs* stored as holographic particles yield deep access and insight to subconscious material normally unconscious. Noetic Field Therapy as an energy medicine modality, directly uses the attributes of the aura in healing and transforming consciousness.

Drug use is apparent in the aura. It is seen clairvoyantly and may be perceived intuitively. Practitioners who have trained their hands to energetic sensitivity can perceive drug residue and its effects and presence by combing the aura.

PART III:

DIMENSIONS OF DRUGS AND CONSCIOUSNESS

Current psychedelic research must expand its viewpoint, leave the mechanistic, linear, closed-ended Newtonian Worldview and enter the holistic quantum lens of perception to see the full picture regarding the effects and usefulness of marijuana derivatives and psychedelics when used medicinally, therapeutically, and spiritually. Having a holistic awareness takes us over a threshold into new frontiers of awareness that will irrevocably change our perception of ourselves as human beings and how we approach science and medicine! Make the leap.

Winston Hampton

Chapter 8:

My Marijuana Experiences

"Learning the language of the human energy system is a means to self- understanding, a way through your spiritual challenges."

Caroline Myss, Ph.D., *Anatomy of the Spirit*

As I write this, marijuana is plastered all over the news. The miracle drug and its legalization are being celebrated left, right, and center. Wow! Back in my stoner days, I would have loved how mainstream pot has become. While I support the legal changes, I know too much about hidden effects to celebrate. Now it's even more important that the deeper, hidden effects become known.

I know the marijuana high like the back of my hand. I loved getting stoned during my drug days. I started my journey embracing drug culture as a huge adventure. I saw God in my psychedelic trips.

I formed my life around self-medicating by constantly staying stoned. Then I found myself having to beat addiction. As much as I loved it, there came a time to move on. Through it all, I desperately sought spiritual experiences in my life.

Remember What?

We would be high as a kite! My friends and I would head for the kitchen – munchies, right? At the bottom of the stairs turn left, go around the corner, and head into the kitchen. Whoops, we're in the dining room. What were we doing there? It was hilarious, we couldn't remember what we were doing!

If you're a stoner, you know what I'm talking about. One thing marijuana does is kill short-term memory. This happened to us a lot. I would walk into one room and forget why I was there in the first place. It's like senior citizen senility. Sound scary? When you're high on THC it's not! I would laugh hysterically at this.

Marijuana is a stress reliever. The mind gets carefree and relaxed, except if you're one of those people who get paranoid on pot. Being stress-free became my priority, and I knew just how to do it -- get high. Memory loss is part of this. I couldn't stress over what I didn't remember.

I failed the 9th grade and dropped out in the 11th grade. I lacked the focus, ambition, and interest to continue my school studies. I was nicely stoned for an entire decade. As time went by, I noticed my memory loss even when I wasn't high. Once I reached my twenties, I noticed how bad my memory was compared to the people around me. My short-term memory was so weak. It was a wake-up call for me. The schoolwork then and in the coming years was difficult to handle while struggling with memory loss.

My family and friends joke about my memory loss. My kids know it and poke fun at it. People tell me their names, and I typically forget them 10 seconds later. I needed a Day-Timer to remind me of my responsibilities.

Although I stopped toking in my early twenties my memory loss stayed with me for a long time. I had to create ways to remember things. During my training in energy medicine and aura balancing, I learned how marijuana affects the magnetic energy fields around the brain and body. I learned how energetic effects caused memory loss. There are biological effects also. The biological and energetic go hand in hand.

For me, the hidden effects taking place in my energy field became crucial to learn about. Given my spiritual focus, it was especially important. I was learning to look with holistic eyes. I began to comprehend how marijuana affected my spiritual path. I began to understand how it affected my health and consciousness in ways I hadn't considered.

It's very interesting that, after I started my spiritual practice, my memory slowly began to improve. I began to notice Spirit's *radiant energies* flow into my mind and body when I meditated or did a form of spiritual focus. When this happened, my memory would improve. As I have aged, my memory has gotten better rather than worse. Fascinating.

My spiritual focus and study made me holistically aware of how universal living intelligence entered into all my levels. As an energy field, it naturally balances, straightens, and heals in diverse ways and levels. Not only did my memory improve but also other faculties.

24 and Stuck At 14

As mentioned, a marijuana high can be a huge stress reliever. I remember as an older teen, always going to my stone when things got rough. There was so much anxiety and angst I went through as a teenager and getting high relieved that. Getting high gave me direct emotional relief. A counselor I worked with later called it self-medication.

When I was high my emotions would phase out and calm down. Also, things got extremely funny. It's interesting how seemingly traumatic situations became funny. Once I watched one of my friends crash on his bicycle. It was hilarious! NOT! He was badly hurt. Disconnect?

Overall, I glided through my teenage years and mostly didn't need to deal with any painful emotional issues. Marijuana nicely glazed over it all. During the decade I was high, I didn't have any issues with my emotional maturity. My constant buzz was like waxing my skis. I just slid through life with few worries.

After seven years of getting high, some negative experiences crept in. It started when I lived in Japan and got my first Thai stick. Pot in the 1960s and 70s generally wasn't all that strong. But Thai stick! EEYOW! It was kick-ass stuff, like what you get on the market today. I started to experience anxiety and paranoia when I got high. Oh man, did that suck!

What I am getting around to is what my experience was after I quit using. As I said before, I stopped because my drive to connect spiritually shook me. While I dealt with on-and-off cocaine addiction, my need for marijuana was a major monkey. I had trouble functioning well without getting high every day. In turn, my natural emotional balance was shit.

Anyway, I quit using drugs and started an intense metaphysical counseling program at Southwestern College* in New Mexico. I needed to be sober to get into the program. Damn, as soon as I stopped using, my emotions started going all over the place.

I was tense, hyperactive, and easily reactive. I depended on marijuana to handle my emotions. This period was awfully hard. Thank goodness I had great community support and had started doing lots of spiritual exercises (meditation).

I didn't know how to handle my emotions. I had no idea how to deal with stuff. I was a psychedelic yo-yo. In a counseling program, you are required to do a lot of introspection, self-work – what I call ego-work – and counseling. I was 23 when I began to learn how to deal with my emotions.

*Southwestern College: is a fully accredited master's degree-granting counseling program. See the Glossary for more info.

In counseling sessions as the client, as I began working on the issues that came up, I had an astounding realization! OMG!! As issues came to be worked on, I realized, "That's the exact issue I had with my dad when I was 14 years old." Or "That's the exact issue I had trying to make myself study in junior high school." Or "That's the same issue I had with my girlfriend when I was fifteen."

What?! I was now working through my early teenage issues. Some of them were incredibly specific. I realized that being stoned all the time somehow put them on hold. All those years I got to slide were coming back around. Those years stoned amounted to avoidance with no resolutions. I spent the next six or seven years in catch-up mode with my emotional maturity.

In my college studies, I learned about the stages of human development as we grow and mature. Emotional development is a crucial part of the process. Learning to handle our emotions is a huge part of becoming a successful adult. I realized pot smoking placed my emotional development on hold.

Southwestern College's counseling program, where I studied, was very metaphysical. At the same time, I met my spiritual teacher and began my spiritual training. The ego work and the spiritual training went hand in hand. I found my spiritual evolution required a healthy engagement with my ego work.

My studies at this time were much more than mental-level learning. Teachers at the school were amazing consciousness instructors in their own right. All of us, students and teachers, were fully engaged in spiritual practices. The core focus was on the transformation of consciousness. We were exploring levels of consciousness and methods of consciousness transformation. My growing awareness of myself as living consciousness was much more than learning theories and memorizing information.

The school exemplified the new education format for these times – experiential education. In other words, direct experience is the path to knowing. I became more aware of my consciousness in the web of life. I became aware of myself as an energetic being. As I learned to do the transformation work with others it fully included the energetic and spiritual aspects of who we are.

I also trained in Noetic Field Therapy (NFT) or **Noetic (aura) Balancing***. Noetic Balancing is a powerful energy medicine modality to holistically transform consciousness. The hands-on training included a detailed study of human energy anatomy. As I progressed in my training, I perceived what emotional stunting, resulting from marijuana use, looks like energetically in consciousness. The energetic perspective or quantum view discloses what a marijuana high looks like in the aura, chakra centers, and energy bodies.

The energetic view allows effects and conditions in the human energy bodies to be seen. These effects and conditions are before and simultaneous with psychological effects, feelings, or states.

*Noetic Balancing or NFT: see details in the Glossary.

A quantum view sees more than just the individual consciousness. It sees the individual as a nested holographic particle within universal oneness, within the living intelligence of the web of life. Energetic effects enhance or block our relationship with Oneness.

Newtonian philosophy has created a culture of suppression. We have adapted to a culture of suppression. Our culture has become a pill-popping, instant-relief society. I experienced marijuana as a suppression drug when used to self-medicate. There is a huge downside. Suppression blocks spiritual progression.

I'm Not Motivated

Recent scientific studies show that THC affects the area of the brain holding motivation. You don't need to be a scientist to know that. You can be a pothead like I was and know by direct experience.

While drug experiences may bring revelations, some experiences are subtle, and effects only show up over time. It took me a few years of getting high to notice my diminishing motivation. After all, I was hanging out in the no worry, be happy place.

Being a heavy user came with strings attached. I avoided 9 to 5 jobs. I managed my stress by staying on the 'high' road. After a while, my friends and I noticed we weren't ambitious about much of anything while high. We just coasted, and that was fine with us.

Like a submarine, my motivation slowly took a nosedive during my years of pot use. Go figure! I'm a high-energy person. I interpreted my lack of motivation as a spiritual sign I was finding peace. My friends and I weren't interested in a career or doing anything substantial with our lives while we were busy getting high.

The marijuana high is very sneaky. I became addicted to the euphoric feeling. The feel-good aspect is so powerful. I started letting things go in my world. I'd rather get high. The memory loss, static emotions, and lack of motivation snuck up on me. The hallmark condition of a THC high is the illusion that everything is just fine.

In stark contrast, when I am in a high spiritual state of consciousness, I experience resilience and flexibility. I see clearly. My coping mechanisms effortlessly take me through the world in an uplifting way. My emotions are perceptions supporting me. My emotional reactions are stepping stones rather than stumbling blocks.

The three primary psychological effects of chronic marijuana use I experienced were:

- My short-term memory was shot.
- My emotional development shut down, but I didn't notice this until after I quit using.
- My motivation kept decreasing.

After quitting drugs and finding an effective spiritual practice I discovered highs without drugs. The natural energy of who we are is clean, clear, and boundless. I see this presence when I watch children playing. My spiritual practice opened places inside me to allow the flow of my Authentic Self. I realized it was a huge relief to get high on loving and Spirit rather than a drug.

A spiritual high is quite different than a suppressed state of consciousness where drugs feed euphoria to my nervous system. Rather than the illusion that all is well, a spiritual high is a reality where I am present, on purpose, and naturally joyful. I don't need to wonder how I'm doing. I know how I'm doing. Hallmarks of spiritual consciousness are self-empowerment, clarity, purpose, joy, enthusiasm, and loving.

Chapter 9:
Marijuana Energy Field Effects

"The addiction to sensation is one of the most subtle. When you become accustomed to sensation, you often feel as if there's something wrong when there is simply a lack of sensation. But sensation is an aspect of the lower levels; the higher levels do not have sensation as we identify it here. So it's important to drop the belief that there must be sensation for something to be happening. There can be action and movement without sensation."

John-Roger, DSS, *Walking with The Lord*

Newtonian scientists take a biochemical approach to research, such as processes within the endocannabinoid system*. They are not able to include the holistic, spiritual-energetic portion of human consciousness. That wouldn't be 'scientific.' However, human consciousness is not linear, it is multi-dimensional and multi-directional. Our biology is actually the lesser part of consciousness.

*Endocannabinoid system: Science calls the various alkaloids, such as THC or CBD, in marijuana cannabinoids. They are naturally occurring lipid-based neurotransmitters. As researchers studied marijuana effects, they observed cannabinoids interacting with the brain and nervous system. They call this system of chemical interaction the endocannabinoid system.

Marijuana affects our consciousness in multiple directions. Its chemicals prompt biochemical cascades. In turn, these cause changes in the energy fields. Substance frequencies also directly affect the energy bodies, organs, and membranes, which causes biological effects. Multi-directional.

The use of marijuana is not usually known to bring Threshold Experiences (see chapter 11) like psychedelics, though initial highs may produce perceptual experiences never before experienced. Such as tasting color or hearing light.

If using medical marijuana for specific health issues, there might be a reduction in stress, pain, seizures, and nausea with an increase in appetite. Some pot alkaloids affect specific physical health conditions to an extent. These positive properties may outweigh any downsides when used by people suffering from cancer, AIDS, seizures, or severe psychopathologies. With medical marijuana, THC* is often the main catalyst for these effects.

Marijuana's effect makes us feel happy and mellow. Our general thought patterns are interrupted or altered, which we experience as a release of worry. That being said, we may be more aware of things in the background.

Our short-term memory is briefly disrupted. We may feel

---

*THC: Tetrahydrocannabinol is the major psychoactive component and one of 113 cannabinoids recognized in cannabis. CBD: Cannabidiol, another primary cannabinoid.

warm, fuzzy, sleepy, or exhilarated. Interestingly, marijuana, like other anti-anxiety drugs, can *also* cause anxiety.

When marijuana is used to get high, all the alkaloids in the plant play a part. My experiences and observations are based on recreational use. The primary ingredient is THC. When the whole plant is used, who can say exactly which cannabinoid does what? CBD is known to buffer the THC effects somewhat. CBD used on its own is a different story. The following information applies to whole plant use.

Auric Snowstorm

Now, let's look at energy field effects. When looking psychically at marijuana in an auric energy field it appears as a whitish or grey static blanket like a snowstorm. It dims the normal clarity and brightness of auric colors. It's mostly comprised of THC frequency. This thick, fuzzy cover surrounds the whole body, especially around the torso and upper part of the body. When combing with the hands it is perceived as a sticky, cottony layer two inches to two feet from the physical body.

The static quality is also caused by the polluted mixing of energy fluids or frequencies. The THC frequency causes rips, tears, and loss of integrity in energy membranes between energy bodies and in chakra centers. This allows leakage and mixing of energy frequencies (each body vibrates at a different frequency) to contaminate the auric field. The static quality of suppressed or blocked energy flow is responsible for a large part of feeling 'high.'

The marijuana frequency suppresses and blocks the healthy flow dynamic of energy, especially through the emotional body. This is one effect people love about the high. The warm fuzziness and soothing of our anxiety result from suppressed energy flow in the emotional/causal body as well as biochemical effects. Energy field flow slows or stops, sensations enhance, and feelings are buffered.

Typically, if someone starts smoking pot at age 14 and uses it steadily up until they are 24, their emotional intelligence (EQ) could be stuck at around fourteen. That was my experience. The 24-year-old is left processing emotional issues they didn't deal with as part of their normal growth and maturation. While someone in their mid-twenties or older may not be developmentally delayed, emotional issues suppressed by pot smoking still need to be resolved later.

As Noetic balancers, we find that if we work with a client to clear a particular mental-emotional issue, we typically must clear the deadening caused by marijuana before we access the actual issue. Marijuana frequencies bring limitations into the human energy field. Trained practitioners use energy to clear, balance, and heal limitations. *Radiant energies* come into the Noetic balancing, easily and gracefully clearing and balancing the limiting energy fields.

If the Conscious Self chooses to get 'high' all the time, processes that are part of the healthy, naturally unfolding, and maturing of consciousness get suppressed. Emotional suppression may interfere with the natural course of experience, resolution, maturation, and basic understanding of life.

There are marijuana users who immediately experience anxiety so intense they are unable to continue using. I view this as a wake-up call for that person. The anxiety may relate to emotional suppression or could be damage to energetic organs.

When THC suppresses the natural healthy flow in the emotional body, consciousness naturally begins to call out for freedom. Anxiety is a messenger. The High Self and Basic Self begin to "provoke" the Conscious Self. Anxious, depressed, and paranoid feelings are always a call for change.

Depending on usage, THC might have a tearing effect on membranes, the etheric body, and the subconscious. Some tearing is centered near the brain's reticular formation corresponding to the pituitary gland. High anxiety, fear, or occasional paranoia is a result of this tearing. Healthy and natural flow cycles in the subconscious can be blocked.

Magnetic Field Disruption

Marijuana has profound effects on our magnetic field dynamics. For example, a natural magnetic energy loop occurs in the aura from the throat area, over the head, to the middle of the back. It gets disrupted by the marijuana frequency. A tear in the etheric body just behind the head, corresponding to the reticular formation in the brain, begins to appear.

This magnetic field is part of Bodymind* and holds information as memory. This magnetic field disruption is specifically why short-term memory retention is interrupted. It's a main reason why a pot smoker may experience 'no worries.'

Recent studies show delayed and stunted development in brain tissue of pot smokers under twenty-five (see *Journal of Neuroscience* in the bibliography.). Newtonian science identifies the chemical compounds in marijuana as the cause, slowing brain tissue growth during developmental ages.

From an energetic perspective, the healthy functioning of the magnetic energy loop is essential to normal, healthy tissue growth. When the loop is inhibited by marijuana use, the development of physical structures is suppressed.

Hallmark of Illusion

Marijuana users experience, to varying degrees, loss of motivation. This relates to direction and purpose along with adverse effects on the subconscious track. Marijuana effectively distorts the perceptions of a life challenge, our experience of the challenge, and the effective resolution of the challenge. Because pot distorts our perception, it displaces spiritual alignment with the *illusion* of alignment.

---

*Bodymind: is a holistic principle. It infers body and mind as one integrated unit. In this case, retention of memory takes place not just in the brain but throughout the whole body.

Marijuana seems to exemplify the neurotransmitter and energetic effects that block anxiety and stress. That was my experience during most of the time I was self-medicating with pot. The blanket that marijuana causes in the overall energy field is smooth and soft in all ways (except when it causes anxiety for a person). The elimination of anxiety and stress feels 'natural'. There aren't really any red flags to let you know you are in an illusion field. Thus, the illusion field is wholly seductive.

The illusion that all is well and perfect is a hallmark of the marijuana high. People love the warm, fuzzy illusion that all is well. This illusion called to me over and over, and I loved it when I was using marijuana to self-medicate. The illusion field is quite powerful and distorts awareness, so you don't notice your movement toward transformation and growth is sidetracked and on hold.

Radiant Energy Blocked

Psychic sight can be forced when the natural protective seals within the chakra centers no longer cohesively function. Increases in psychic awareness by psychotropic drugs happen when chakras are forced open.

The magnetic frequency of THC is like a lid placed over the consciousness. From my spiritually oriented perspective, perhaps the most negative effect of marijuana use is the way it blocks the connection to higher-frequency spiritual energies. There is something about the THC frequency that inhibits the inflow of *radiant energies* normally entering consciousness through the crown and brow chakras. In this way, it hampers spiritual awareness. It gives the illusory experience of spiritual connection.

Spiritually sourced *radiant energy* frequencies bring balance, alignment, and clarity throughout our bodies. This translates into a psychological experience of greater mental and emotional clarity as well as clarity of purpose. The aura takes on greater luminescence with clearer, brighter, and more profound colors.

The inflow of *radiant energies* supports health and well-being. Their nature is to bring balance and transformation to all our levels mental, emotional, and spiritual. Over time, this results in the elimination of anxieties, fear, and depression, among other conditions. The conditions causing these imbalances are brought into balance and healed.

Sometimes, as the higher spiritual frequencies free up bound *energetic constructs*, they cause healing crises in one or more levels in our consciousness. Sometimes they release the next set of life path challenges. *Radiant energies* know and honor, to the highest degree, our life path and our highest good. *Radiant energies* know this far beyond our conscious awareness.

The *choice* to use THC recreationally multiplies the block to higher-frequency spiritual energies. Making this choice includes giving over part of our inner authority to a substance and its Spirit Guardian. This opens the door to influences in our consciousness that may not serve our highest good. These include sabotaging the subconscious, promoting a loss of purpose, and losing integrity & motivation.

Anti-depressants have similar energetic effects, although not as pervasive as marijuana. Anti-depressants and similar prescribed drugs do not block *radiant energies* the same way as marijuana. They are typically prescribed and used with the intent to bring greater balance. Their use has little negative effect until it clearly becomes a suppression or addiction.

Chapter 10:
Psychedelic Experience

"If the Zero Point Field were included in our conception of the most fundamental nature of matter, they realized, the very underpinning of our universe was a heaving sea of energy—one vast quantum field. If this were true, everything would be connected to everything else like some invisible web."

Lynn McTaggert, *The Field*

In this chapter, I briefly share my entry into and my experiences in high-dose psychedelic sessions. My mystical experiences during high-dose sessions have givern me references to similar or identical mystical states and transcendence resulting from spiritual practices.

These experiences laid the groundwork for my firsthand realization of how psychoactive drugs affect the human energy field. I was quite young when I started my psychedelic explorations. I most definitely wouldn't recommend it to anyone with what I know now. Still, this was my journey.

During puberty, I had a big awareness shift. I became self-aware in a whole new way. This was a real insight for me and profound at the time. I came into a new level of self-consciousness. Imminently important questions about life followed. Who am I? What was my purpose on Earth? What was the purpose of life?

I wasn't interested in hearing I was a 13-year-old kid named Winston who lived with his parents at a certain address … Blah. As young as I was, I wanted answers to cosmic and existential questions bothering me. I asked my parents. Their answers were not helpful. I spoke to a minister at church and got rote-learned dogma from him. He didn't have the answers I was looking for either.

I wasn't sure what answer I was looking for. I wanted a response that would transcend my normal, little life. I didn't know at the time I was beginning my search for spiritual meaning. Information was ultimately not what I was looking for. I sought direct experience. I wanted a *knowing* that only comes from direct experience.

At the same time, I was super self-conscious and possessed big-time self-esteem issues. I was very unsure of myself. There were stressors on top of that. Growing up, my family moved every couple of years. My dad worked for an oil company. As a geologist, he was learning the geology of different areas of the country. Moving was hard on me. A new school and new friends every year or so. I had a lot of anxiety.

As a young teen, I think my curiosity about life coupled with stress led me to explore an alternative side of life. I smoked my first joint at 14. I suppose peer and cultural pressure contributed to this. My first pot high was profound. I experienced synesthesia, which is when your sense perceptions cross over and mix, like tasting color, or hearing pictures in your mind's eye.

I could taste color. Wow!

I noticed my worries faded when I smoked pot and a wave of relief washed over me. My inhibitions weakened as I entered a state of euphoria. What I needed was self-medication, and I loved it. Over time I toyed with nearly every substance one can get high on to test their effects on me. For my friends and me, smoking pot was definitely a smooth way to self-medicate.

It was the 1960s and 70s. The 'Flower Power' and 'Love-In' movements rocked the nation. Hippies were a colorful and seductive happening. They fought against the status quo and stood for a new way of being. They reveled in the metaphysical experiences of getting high and made love openly. I wanted to be one of them.

At 15 years young, in 1970, I decided to try other drugs beyond marijuana. I decided to go on the adventure of opening doors with a group of friends to explore the psychedelic experience. We set out on an unknown journey to, hopefully, discover the secrets to life. This became a central focus for me over the next several years. I dropped out of school in my junior year, tuned in, turned on, and dropped out.

At that point in our young lives, we experimented with psychedelics like peyote/mescaline, LSD*, STP, DMT, and psilocybin mushrooms. Psychedelics we had access to were relatively pure. When in a natural form like mushrooms or peyote, it's naturally pure. We got our purest stuff from a local underground chemist. Pretty quickly, we moved from a recreational approach to a sacramental level.

It's well known that 'set and setting' are crucial to the trip. 'Setting' is the environment, social scene, cultural influences, and rituals. We chose the woods as a natural, quiet setting where we wouldn't be bothered. We made camp with tents.

'Set' is the state of mind and personality of the individual. We tripped as a group supporting one another. We left our worldly concerns behind as much as possible. As a guide, I helped steer the trip to stay more elevated.

---

*LSD: Powerful psychedelic/psychotropic drugs affecting the consciousness with very low doses. LSD: lysergic sour(acid) diethylamide synthesized from ergot (mold). Slow onset. 10–12-hour trip. STP: 2,5-Dimethoxy-4-methylamphetamine, nicknamed Serenity, Tranquility, and Peace. Slow onset. 12–16-hour trip. DMT: N, N-Dimethyltryptamine occurs in many plants and animals including humans. Ayahuasca, Toad Medicine. Rapid onset, short duration.

LSD and mescaline were my favorites. STP was hard to get. Psilocybin mushrooms were more flowery and didn't seem to have a direct deep dive. DMT was quite different. It seemed more superficial to me and, again, not as deep. LSD was a clean, more streamlined path. Mescaline went deep and had a strong connection to the natural world.

We took the drugs, closed our eyes, and went inside. Often, we would spend hours meditating and exploring inner landscapes. We had unified group perceptions, both inner and outer. We did some amount of sharing out loud during the trip, and more after reentry. This was our ritual. We traveled inside our consciousness to explore and see what we could find. For me, mystical experiences started happening right away.

One of my journal entries from 1972: *"There we were on the levee, next to the Mighty Muddy Mama, the Mississippi River. We were having an atavistic experience. We knew that, as humans, we had been sitting on the banks of rivers for, perhaps, a million years, taking the leap into the unknown. In our case, dropping a very high dose of mescaline and going in. Our heartbeats throbbed the beat of Universal Life. We were the skin stretched tight on the Drum of Life. This ancient sound of our blood pumping through our veins was taking us out into the Cosmos. I experienced the great No-Thingness. I was merging with the great Nothingness. Would I survive this? My ego was deathly afraid as I entered into the heartbeat of life."*

PSYCHEDELICS, TRANSCENDENCE AND SPIRITUALITY

As I was propelled by each high-dose psychedelic experience, my consciousness would go over some kind of threshold into a wholly 'new' awareness level. I came to call this a Threshold Experience. Each voyage over the threshold brought new mind-bending realizations and experiences. In our drug-use-driven culture, we often talk about side effects. Some might say a possible side effect of taking a psychedelic is psychosis. That would be a 'bad' side effect. For me, I ended up with a side effect I thought was rather cool.

I developed psychic abilities that opened me up to see auras and energy fields. I could see the egg-shaped, colorful energy fields around people. I could see colored energy fields around trees, rock formations, and other things in the environment. I also could see into personalities and egos in people everywhere I went.

Psychic sight was awesome, but I was shaken by seeing the personality structures of people I knew. I wanted to shut that ability. The fact I could see those things and talk about them landed me in a mental institution when I was 17. I was in for a couple of months until I escaped. (That's another story.) Ram Dass* warned about having psychedelic mystical experiences and then trying to tell the world about it in his best-selling 1971 book *Be Here Now*.

*Ram Dass (Richard Alpert) was a Ph.D. professor who became a psychedelic guru in the 1960s with Timothy Leary. Alpert went to India in 1967, met his spiritual guru, and became Ram Dass. He went on to become a well-known American spiritual teacher. He died in 2019 at age 88.

During my days of nonstop drug intake, I wasn't aware of the invisible effects accompanying high-dose trips. Newtonian science would call these side effects. These effects are deeply interconnected to all that is uplifting about psychedelic experiences. The effects I refer to are those in the human energy field. They may not show up for months or years. There were energetic changes and therefore psychological changes I remained unaware of for quite some time. I discuss this in detail in chapters 12 and 13.

I also saw the underbelly of the drug culture in which I was immersed. I saw people who were pounded and burned by their drug adventures. Some lost their lives or had emotional and mental breakdowns. Others had long-term psychological challenges and struggled to live balanced, fulfilled lives. For the psychedelic users I knew, sustainable and meaningful change rarely, if ever, took place in their daily lives.

Native or indigenous traditions include consciousness (spiritual) education in their plant medicine ritual use. For example, ayahuasca ceremonial use emphasizes personal and spiritual development, the acquisition of knowledge, and the improvement of interpersonal relationships. The Native American Peyote Church teaches guidance from a higher power with teachings about healing personal, social, and communal issues.

There is a sustainable positive effect I want to mention here. I received Reference Points from these high-dose sessions that deeply altered my worldview. These gave me direct experiences of a quantum world.

Psychedelic experiences are filled with multi-level energy flows and fields. I experienced myself as an energetic being. I experienced the universe and world made of energy. Knowing myself and life as energy was a new, profound lens of perception. Later, this became a building block in my spiritual studies and study of energy medicine.

After four years with psychedelics, I began to experience some adverse side effects. I experienced times of mental and emotional instability. One of my most pronounced challenges was dissociation. It felt like parts of me were disconnected from other parts. I felt ungrounded and my perception of reality would shimmer like heat waves over a hot road. These kinds of psychological challenges persisted even after I quit using drugs.

Then, of course, there is the danger of habit. As time went by, I became synonymous with drugs and hung out with other users more and more. Schoolwork was a major turnoff. Getting high became my priority. "Don't worry, be happy" became my mantra. I just needed to smoke a joint to let the good times roll. Later, marijuana became the hardest drug for me to quit. The high and the act of getting high became ingrained in my subconscious.

Underlying my drug explorations was my search for meaning. I did more than just do drugs during this period. I also read everything I could find on drugs and their effects. It made sense to learn all I could. I wanted to learn the pros and cons of each psychotropic. There was plenty of propaganda, half-truths, and falsities to wade through. Also, nothing was published on energy field effects. There is still very little published on human energy field effects.

My psychedelic exploration included other avenues in my search to understand and know Spirit (consciousness). I desperately wanted to wake my spirituality and tap its internal power to answer my most pressing questions. I read metaphysical books and scripture, including the Bible, to quench my thirst for knowledge. I read the Hindu *Bhagavad Gita*, the *Tao of Lao Tzu*, and anything on Buddhism, especially the Zen form of the practice.

I wanted more, so I moved to publications on meditation, yoga, and spirituality. I tried 'awakening methods' from all kinds of places. Methods of awakening are practices like meditation, chanting, fasting, prayer, doing yoga, and so on. Eventually, I began the search for a teacher. I wanted one who could guide me toward a direct experience of spiritual consciousness. I continued to be less interested in information and wholly wanted direct experiences.

In my early 20s, my drug idealism turned to addiction. At 23, I knew I needed to move on. I couldn't seem to recapture the original experiences of mysticism and wonder. I felt held down by drugs at this point. They were like a monkey on my back. My wheels were spinning but I wasn't going anywhere. I turned my attention to my spiritual questions.

Ram Dass said, *"There are three stages in this journey that I have been on! The first, the social science stage; the second, the psychedelic stage; and the third, the yogi stage."* For me, my advancement through the stages happened very early in life, I was ready for the yogi stage. I call it my spiritual education stage.

At 23, as I let go of the drug world, I went back to school and studied for a master's degree in counseling. Part of my next years of education included training in **Energy Medicine** or **Vibrational Medicine**. I experientially learned human energy anatomy, auras, chakra centers, and many aspects of the human energy field. I learned aura balancing or Noetic Balancing.

I had enormous realizations in those next years. For instance, though I knew I had valuable Reference Points from my high-dose psychedelic experiences, I didn't have any sustainable transformation in my day-to-day life. I came to see any long-lasting positive change from psychedelic use *had* to include consciousness education. Psychology calls this Cognitive Behavioral Education (CBE).

I first met my spiritual teacher in a dream on inner spiritual realms and then later met him physically. He was a true spiritual teacher who worked with his students in ways that brought transformation on all levels. He showed me many, many keys to spiritual awakening. He demonstrated how to clear karma, expand awareness, how to reach into transcendence, and how to do spiritual exercises that worked. In the coming years we met often on the inner realms and occasionally in the world. I began to enter direct experiences of the divine I was seeking.

Over time my training and learning reached higher levels. I came to see, in my experience, how our physical and biochemical anatomy are wholly interconnected with our energy anatomy. Each physical organ and system has a corresponding energy organ and system. Conditions within our physical biochemistry are caused by or take place first in the energy bodies, organs, and systems.

I no longer saw the physical world and my physical self as material form. I became aware of the state of reality that physicists talk about. A tree is a construct of molecules made up of atoms that are simply whirling particles. The world and who we are, are forms of manifested energy. My lens of perception was now an energetic lens.

I now see psychological states as expressions of energetic conditions. Our psychological states are felt-sensed experiences of energetic conditions. This energetic perception of the whole human deeply informs what I share about the more invisible and, challenging to identify, effects of psychotropic drug use.

This training and awareness, along with my spiritual path, reveal point-blank how drugs affect us energetically. I share hidden truths, the deeper effects of drugs on our spiritual path, and growth. They are hidden because they are invisible and difficult to pinpoint. I'll explain what goes on in your aura and chakra centers when you get high. I'll share possible long-term psychological effects of high-dose psychedelic use.

I learned hidden truths about the price we pay when we use marijuana to self-medicate and when we use psychedelics as a shortcut to transcendental experience. I learned there are fundamental differences between drug-induced psychedelic transcendence and naturally occurring transcendence.

Chapter 11:
Psychedelic Dynamics

"Furthermore, keep in mind that a spirit molecule is not spiritual in and of itself. It is a tool or a vehicle. Think of it as a tugboat, a chariot, a scout on horseback, something to which we can hitch our consciousness. It pulls us into worlds known only to itself. We need to hold on tight, and we must be prepared, for spiritual realms include both heaven and hell, both fantasy and nightmare. While the spirit molecule's role may seem angelic, there is no guarantee it will not take us to the demonic."

Rick Strassman, M.D. *The Spirit Molecule*

During my seven-year psychedelic expedition, the session sequence became quite familiar to me. The process became ingrained after a while. Being a tour guide pushed me to know the way even more. In the midst of these experiences, and in retrospect, it was helpful to identify the dynamics of high-dose sessions.

The dynamics are the sequence and distinct activities taking place within the experience. These dynamics hold true for everyone on a typical high-dose trip. Here is an outline that creates a basic framework of the practical principles of the journey.

I think the dynamics of high-dose psychedelic sessions are helpful to know. We are developing a common language for the experience. Every researcher and trip guide can make use of knowing these. They do not apply to micro-dosing.

- Doors of Perception
- Threshold Experience
- Transcendence
- Psychedelic Ceiling
- Pattern Interruption
- Ego Bypass
- Coming Down
- Reference Points

The **doors of perception** identify the shift from a normal frame of perception to an altered and expanded one. Depending on what and how you imbibe the psychedelic the timing may be immediate or occur in an hour or two.

The doors didn't merely open for me. I was kicked head over heels through them. A whole new world opened. I would Soul-gaze at the beauty of clouds and leaves for hours at a time. I saw color as if I had never noticed it before. Their shades become vibrant and alive.

Vision, taste, feeling, and sound take on new scale and meaning. Seeing, hearing, and tactile sensations offer multi-levels of meaning. There are worlds within worlds within worlds in a blue flower or a cricket chirping.

Our personalities create a many-layered worldview to survive. This becomes our personal lens of perception. Psychedelics offer a way to journey past our normal lens into a whole new world. The possible profound life learnings are exciting prospects for researchers and visionaries.

As time went by, I identified perceptions on biological, cellular, atomic, and subatomic levels. It's fascinating how awareness can be macro or micro. Perception into these levels is like entering different universes. It's challenging to discern whether you're traveling through your body as an infinitesimally small spark of awareness or actually experiencing another dimension.

In the years following my high-dose experiences, as I had more and more mystical, transcendent experiences without drugs, I developed Reference Points. I could now identify past trip experiences.

I was traveling through the cell level in my body.

Or I went past the cell level into a molecular level.

Or this experience was when I passed the physical veil and entered into the astral realm.

The visuals, colors, and feeling tones are clearly astral. Once I assisted a fellow tripper out of his bad trip. I followed him into the hellish lower astral and brought him out.

To know and distinguish these awarenesses requires clear discernment in perception. I didn't acquire this discernment during high-dose sessions. At that time all was new, the intense experiences were explorations of undiscovered territory. Later, explorations of altered states of awareness through a spiritual practice brought discernment of where I was traveling in my consciousness within the multiverse of life. That, and the guidance of a master consciousness who had full awareness of where consciousness was traveling at any moment.

As the psychedelic takes effect and an altered state of consciousness expands, there is a point where experience passes a threshold. This threshold is beyond the sensory expansion in perception. It is a distinct point in the session I call a **Threshold Experience**.

After crossing this threshold, we enter experiences that very much transcend our normal lens. If a session lasts 10 hours, the threshold is around two to four hours in. There is a peak to the psychedelic journey at around five to six hours in and may last for a couple of hours.

When I crossed the threshold, I realized I was no longer in control. I had moments of fear and even terror. Then I began entering into what I call a mystical experience.

Sometimes there were profound visual experiences. Beautiful detailed geometric mandala patterns opened in my inner vision. When I focused on any part of it a whole new pattern emerged that was unique, colorful, and radiant. This became a movement of opening, over and over. This occurred infinitely. I sat and observed this for hours on end. It felt like I was traveling.

In this altered state over the threshold, I entered universal consciousness. The wisdom teaching of unity just naturally embraced me. I saw, felt, and experienced the web of life and the interconnectedness of all things. This vibrated my whole being.

The profound experience was like having blinders removed from my eyes. I experienced myself and the universe as one living, moving, dynamic being. There was no separation. All is One. I deeply experienced the reality of all life as one living organism.

I entered no-time, a state of absolute timelessness. Time was a fabrication of the ego. It did not actually exist. Past and future were illusions.

Upon leaving the illusion field of time, all perception, cognition, and awareness were present here and now. There was nowhere to go and nothing to do except simply be here now. This was a profound and far-reaching realization. The trip hours became timeless. There was an inpouring of information, wisdom, and realizations immeasurable in their scope.

In the midst of my high-dose sessions, I thought my psychedelic experiences brought **Transcendence**. There was a connotation of spiritual advancement. However, the meaning of the word transcendence is broad. The simplest sense of the word refers to a shift from one state of consciousness to another. It's important to clarify this meaning.

What we call transcendence has to be more than just an intense experience. There are too many intense experiences in life that clearly do not fit into the idea of transcending. Over time, I identified what transcendence meant to me.

Transcendence is an altered state of consciousness taking us beyond normal ego limitations and defenses. It may include experiences of invisible, spiritual realms accompanied by mystical realization. There is the presence of mystical ecstasy or bliss.

The value of transcendence is positive uplifting change bringing greater balance, health, and loving with deeper purpose and understanding. Life issues somehow resolve, and the positive change is sustainable.

The idea of transcendence in psychedelic culture is open to misunderstanding and perhaps superstition. One misunderstanding has to do with having the doors of perception thrown open. High-dose psychedelic experiences are intense. Part of the chemical function removes the natural brain/neural inhibition system.

There is a huge increase in sensory perception. This increase might be 100 times our normal perception. On a high-dose trip, you could spend hours paying attention to stimuli that are normally inhibited. For example, staring at a leaf for hours. Some people decide that increased perception equals transcendence.

Then there is a more fundamental misunderstanding based on our limited worldview. When mystics, saints, or high spiritual teachers have spontaneous transcendence, we look at it in a certain way. Mystics and saints can be windows into invisible, mysterious realms of Spirit. We may come to their teachings for guidance. We trust their transcendence. As a spiritual scientist I must ask: Is there a difference between psychotropic-induced transcendence and natural or spontaneous transcendence?

My personal journey has included both high-dose, psychedelic-prompted transcendence and spontaneous transcendence. Having had both experiences allows me to perceive a difference. Seeing through quantum eyes allows me to perceive a difference.

I'd like to present a new echelon of understanding about this. I think clarification here is crucial to research and exploration, crucial to placing any value therapeutically and spiritually (See Part IV for more details).

I had threshold experiences for a few years. Eventually, I realized what Ram Dass and Timothy Leary said about them having a ceiling was true. They tried increasing their dosages of LSD to thousands of micrograms in search of more. I hit a **psychedelic ceiling.** I realized LSD could only take me so far. It was becoming a repetition instead of an exploration.

There's a fine line here. Yes, you can absolutely continue to have intense psychedelic experiences. The expansion of sensory perception always increases. Perhaps this ceiling actually defines something for which we are searching. Or, maybe, it's a sign our mindset is approaching it. Perhaps the experience of a ceiling simply exposes the limitations of seeking enlightenment by applying chemicals to our nerve endings.

Another very important dynamic occurs during high-dose sessions. I call it **Pattern Interruption**. After a trip, I noticed shifts in how I thought and did things. I believed it was an expansion of my consciousness.

Our consciousness has patterns, habit patterns, ways we do things, and also biological patterns. There is a reflective relationship biologically (the brain and its system) and energetically (energy field and auric field). Psychotropic substances in high-dose settings cause disruption energetically and biologically.

Habits change. Addiction patterns may not be as before, and emotional and thought patterns may shift. You could think of it as wiping the slate clean and starting fresh. Pattern Interruption happens primarily because of its effects on the subconscious area.

Pattern interruption caused by psychotropic use has a tremendous therapeutic interest. Perhaps we could use drugs to initiate a change. This may lead to clearing our minds and thoughts from unhealthy habits to create healthier behaviors. Theoretically, we could use psychedelics to change patterns and improve learning for people. In turn, people could lead healthier and more positive lives.

However, there is a downside. Psychedelics not only disrupt negative patterns in the mind and subconscious, but positive patterns are also affected. Healthy habits and patterns are just as easily interrupted. This relates to the subconscious and subconscious effects.

Ego Bypass clearly happens during high-dose psychedelic experiences. During the session experience, personality structures and ego protections are nicely sidestepped in a way that is very intriguing. Like other psychedelic explorers, I noticed my ego was completely bypassed. Later, when I came down, my ego returned unchanged.

The way Ego Bypass happens shows how *sustainable* changes to our personality typically do not happen when we take a psychedelic, which is probably a good thing. Sustainable change is made possible by receiving guidance and education during and/or after a trip.

Education is an important ingredient. Educating consciousness is a time-honored sustainable method for transformation. A spiritual practice that is effective teaches and promotes movement from ego-centered to Soul-centered. The process of this movement involves education and is incremental transformation.

The Ego Bypass also demonstrates that our essential awareness is not the ego. The ego is a personality structure within which our essential awareness lives and operates in this world. As spiritual beings, our awareness isn't required to be bound within ego.

My tripping experiences were mystically oriented, maybe because I had such strong spiritual intentions. Psychedelic trips have a beginning, a middle, and an end. You go on a high and need to **Come Down** eventually. Thank goodness. Psychedelic travelers who did not Come Down were generally committed to mental institutions.

Here is what Ram Dass said about this in *Be Here Now*: *"In these few years we had gotten over the feeling that one experience was going to make you enlightened forever. We saw that it wasn't going to be that simple. And for five years I dealt with the matter of "coming down". The coming down matter is what led me to the next chapter of this drama. Because after six years, I realized that no matter how ingenious my experimental designs were, and how high I got, I came down ... And it was a terribly frustrating experience as if you came into the of heaven and you saw how it all was and you felt these new states of awareness, and then you got cast out again, and after 2 or 300 times of this, began to feel an extraordinary kind of depression set in – a very gentle depression that whatever I knew still wasn't enough."*

The greatest value I received from my journey with psychotropics is my **Reference Points**. I didn't experience transformation or permanent change after my sessions. My personality and my habits, both good and bad, were much the same. The intense experience stayed a while, then I always went back to being me. Yet, I received valuable Reference Points that shifted my lens of perception of myself and the world.

My long-lasting and important Reference Points were:

- The experience of spiritual dimensions beyond the physical.
- The experience of unity consciousness.
- The experience of timelessness.
- The experience I was not my ego.

These Reference Points altered my view of death. I saw death differently. I had the Reference Point of transcending the ego illusion of death. I've heard others have this Reference Point also. My fear, stress, and anxiety around death were mostly eliminated. This could be a huge shift and support for the terminally ill.

Chapter 12:
Psychedelic Energy Field Effects

"Wisdom, of course, is easier to obtain in hindsight. In hindsight, it is easy to see that it might have been prudent for Leary and his coterie to wait a number of years before proclaiming the psychedelic experience, in itself, as a fast track to "enlightenment," whatever that is. They might have restrained themselves, observing the longer-term effects of psychedelic use on themselves, their work, and their relationships."

Daniel Pinchbeck, introduction to *"Psychedelic Experience"* by Leary, Alpert, and Metzner

I have actively studied energetic humans for over 40 years. In consciousness, I find the connection and relationship between the biological and energetic to be a fascinating mystery. How does my biological chemistry interconnect with my energetic self to become states of consciousness?

As much as I know about the energetic human, much is still a mystery. I don't know specifically how energetic organs, bodies, and membranes interconnect and function to create states of consciousness.

The specifics I know about psychotropic drug effects on the

human energy field and consciousness are based mostly on direct experience. There are also the observations of my teachers and peers doing Noetic Balancing work. The Association of Noetic Practitioners*, over 40 years, has reviewed, discussed, and verified the findings I share here.

Psychedelics here refer primarily to the psychoactive drugs LSD, STP, DMT-ayahuasca/toad medicine, mescaline-peyote/San Pedro cactus, and psilocybin mushrooms. I don't include MDMA (ecstasy), Ketamine, or PCP (Phencyclidine, Angel Dust) as psychedelics because they are empathogens or dissociative anesthetics and have different experience characteristics. All psychedelics appear to feature similar energy field effects.

Auric Field Effects

The aura is the 'whole' human energy field. It is the energetic manifestation of consciousness. It is the collective of energy frequencies of a physical body and all energy organs, bodies, and membranes comprising human consciousness. The electromagnetic field of the aura reveals inner conditions present within the whole energy field of consciousness.

*Association of Noetic Practitioners: a professional collegial organization of Noetic Balancing practitioners formed to share and educate practical transformation of consciousness findings. Members have completed 4-5 years of training in principles of spirituality and Noetic Balancing.

Psychological states of experience are the felt-sensed expressions of our energy anatomy. Our bodies' conditions – physical, imaginal, emotional, mental, and unconscious – collectively create ongoing psychological experiences. The conditions of our chakra system, etheric template, and energetic membranes contribute to the felt-sensed psychological experience.

In the chapter on marijuana energy field effects, I described how the aura gets a static blanket that looks like a snowstorm. This effect also takes place with psychedelic use. With psychedelics, the energy frequency of the drug adds less, and the polluted mixing of body or organ frequencies adds more. There is a greater chance of ripping and tearing membranes and chakra centers with a psychedelic because they are a more powerful psychotropic.

Structures and membranes in our physical body keep various fluids separate, which is essential for biological health. Our energy anatomy is identical. When energetic membranes are damaged with tears and holes, energy pollution results. Barbara Brennan called this "etheric mucus." Energetic qualities of the drugs add to this etheric mucus pollution, which is part of the auric snowstorm.

When I used psychedelics, the crash and recovery after a trip were not healthy responses. Taking a psychedelic always depleted me physically. I always needed to recover. After a high-dose session, the aura doesn't appear vibrant and glowing but tired, thin, and opaque.

When I first met my Noetic Balancing teachers following years of drug use, they described the state of my aura in a similar way that Choa Kok Sui, founder of Pranic Healing*, describes damage. It had rips and tears in the auric fabric. Ellavivian Power, one of my consciousness and Noetic Balancing teachers, was clairvoyant and saw auras. She said my aura looked like sheets flapping in the wind.

I had fairly severe damage in my aura resulting from 10 years of drug use. Partaking of psychotropic substances, especially repetitive use causes thinning and may tear holes in various membranes of the energy field. This thinning and tearing is integral to the cause of intense and vivid psychological experiences during a high-dose trip. My etheric body was ripped and torn, allowing energy to leak in and out. Membrane layers and chakra organs were compromised, damaged, and scarred.

Damaged energy body membranes and organs express as specific psychological experiences. Other high-dose pioneers have described headaches centered around the brow chakra or erratic buzzing energy in their nervous system. I experienced forced psychic awareness. I experienced dissociation and recklessness and observed similar challenges in many of my psychedelic-using peers immediately or sometime later.

*Choa Kok Sui (1952-2007) created the modern Pranic Healing system utilizing Pranic or Ki (chi) energy to heal a variety of elements. Chakras play a central role in the healing modality. Prana means life force energy.

Another effect for me was a heightened sharpness and clarity in my consciousness. My inner mental imaginal imagery was brighter, more colorful, and sharper. Heightened spiritual awareness also has this effect but minus the damage.

A person may be neurotic, prone to addiction, and have emotional or mental issues and still function normally to a great degree. Damage to the aura disrupts its harmonizing functions. Disruption of auric cohesion opens a person to more prevalent neurosis, addictive patterns, or emotional issues. Psychological difficulties needing resolution reflect energetic tissues needing repair. Negative patterns can gain power in their influence over a person.

For me, there were underlying patterns that came with the heightened sharpness and clarity. The presence of a less caring, more self-centered attitude was subtle. My energy was quite dynamic during this time, but my risk-taking behavior really increased. There was a wildness and recklessness in my consciousness. I was less and less aligned with maturity and sensibility.

My subconscious dynamics were severely disrupted. Any intelligence I had to help restrain myself from addictive possibilities was foggy. I was more and more prone to take risks with long-term consequences. The positive presence of guardrail patterns in my life path and consciousness was disrupted and dissipated.

Another way I see it is the communication line in my subconscious from High Self to Basic Self to Conscious Self is like a train track. It is clearly laid out and, when functioning well, helps provide purposefulness, direction, and guidance. The psychedelics caused breaks in the track. I now had a propensity for addictive behavior as well as struggles with purpose, motivation, and direction.

Other manifestations of damage may be experiences of unsolicited mood swings with no apparent cause. Panic attacks, free-floating anxiety, and depression could manifest. There may be impending feelings or dream disturbances.

Another primary effect is the experience of dissociation. It is fascinating how our psychological felt-sense experiences reflect actual conditions in the energy body membranes and organs. The aura is struggling to harmonize the various body frequencies. Harmony produces feelings of well-being, purposefulness, and fulfillment. When the various energetic aspects are not harmonizing, they are at odds with one another. They are separated and disconnected. Thus, the feeling of dissociation.

This book addresses human energy field effects in relation to psychedelics. The same conditions and attributes may also be present from any number of other causes. Energy medicine practitioners such as Barbara Brennan, Choa Kok Sui, and many others identified the same kind of damage and condition in the energy field resulting in physical and mental illness.

Chakra Opening

Chakras are organs of transmutation and perception. We live in multiple dimensions simultaneously – physical, imaginal, emotional, mental, and unconscious. These dimensions are filled with people, places, and things just like the physical universe. Each body gives us access into its dimension. The physical body travels the physical worlds, the astral body travels the astral worlds, and so on.

One side effect I experienced from my psychedelic use was I could suddenly see energy fields, auras, and personality patterns. I saw colorful halos around people and things in the environment. My psychic eyes and clairvoyant vision burst open. Chakras are portals and allow us the perception of information in psychic dimensions. Bits and pieces of dubious information invaded my personal space. As time went by, I wanted to block this onslaught of pushy content into my consciousness.

Chakras also contain an energetic damping system mirroring the brain/neural inhibiting function. They screen perceptive experiences of various dimensions as well as thoughts, emotions, fantasies, and energy fields in the psychic environment. Psychedelics force chakra centers to open. When taken in doses large enough to produce a Threshold Experience, the user may describe having veils torn away from their "mind." Again, the experience of veils torn away is a literal action of chakra petals torn open.

When chakra centers are forced open, they may be damaged. The petals that open and close could get stuck. In turn, the organ ends up with rips and tears. When forced open they might be stuck open for a while. We may be left with psychic awareness, which in my case lasted around 20 years.

A primary experience of forced open chakra centers is increased psychic perception. This may be visual, like the ability to see subtle energy fields. Or it could allow access to information normally hidden. Clairvoyants and psychics can open and close their chakra centers at will. This is a healthy and functional ability. Chakras forced open and stuck are dysfunctional.

Dysfunctional psychic openness is perceived as an invasive experience. This material manifests as hallucinations, hearing voices, and invasion of thoughts not your own. and so on. Other psychological experiences resulting from damaged chakra centers are depression, anxiety, general lack of grounding, and dissociation. My observation is that chakra center damage (versus general auric damage) tends to manifest as more severe or intense psychological disturbances.

While this is not really part of my discussion here, chakra center damage is present in many physical illnesses. Disease and illness are usually present in our energy anatomy first before they manifest physically. For example, Barbara Brennan in *Hands of Light* said, *"A torn chakra ... has appeared in every cancer patient I have seen. Again, the configurations listed here go out to the seventh layer. A chakra can be torn, and cancer may not appear in the body until two or more years later. The protective shield is completely ripped away from this chakra."*

The majority of the psychedelic experience is either expanded sensory perception in the physical body, the felt-sensed experience of energy field damage, or psychic perception into the Astral Realm. In *DMT: The Spirit Molecule,* Rick Strassman shared that many of his research subjects experienced the presence of beings during the session. In my experience, beings such as these appearing while tripping are typically those on the Devic (see chapter 14) or astral levels although this is not *always* true.

Some yogic traditions purposefully practice opening psychic centers. Kundalini yoga is one of them. If you study any of these practices, there is a great deal of caution expressed by the yogis.

Opening too fast results in experiences that aren't so fun. Some shamanistic traditions focus on the naval or solar center. When Carlos Castaneda shared Don Juan's teachings, he talked about extraordinary things Yaqui Shamans could do through their Solar Chakras.

Increased psychic perception does not equate with spiritual awareness. There is a general misunderstanding about this due to a lack of discernment in the difference between psychic and spiritual frequencies of energy. Many consider any invisible dimension or being to be spiritual. In the cosmology I present here, psychic energies are based on duality and spiritual energies are singular. In popular culture, they are the same.

In a spiritual practice, physical sensory perceptions act as a veil blocking us from more subtle forms, including psychic. Physical sensory experience forms a fabric that acts as a veil obscuring higher spiritual awareness. When perception opens to psychic worlds, perception is still bipolar magnetic energy forms. Psychic perceptions now form the veil, albeit at a higher-frequency than physical sensory information, but still act as a veil obscuring awareness into spiritual singular energy field worlds.

The magnetic psychic levels reside within dual cause-and-effect, karma-creating worlds. It can be exciting for the ego to claim psychic perception. Yet, it doesn't necessarily equate with spiritual progression. Spiritual awareness takes place through the Authentic Self. Chakras are involved, the top third of the brow chakra and the crown chakra. Spiritual awareness relates to the singular energy fields above the dual magnetic fields.

Master spiritual teachers teach us to avoid psychoactive substances if we are serious about our spiritual growth (consciousness teachers teach many things including the use of psychotropics.) They see that, while psychedelics may open some doors, there is a strong probability, over time, the drugs cause damage that ends up interfering with our evolution. Or they promote habits that later get in our way.

My spiritual teacher saw this. He taught me to find and apply an effective spiritual practice using time-honored methods to bring transformation and promote access to transcendental states of awareness. Effective spiritual practice naturally includes ego work, bringing balance, healing, and expansion to the ego, resulting in sustainable consciousness transformation.

Radiant energies are part of such a practice, coming present in their innate wisdom to foster progression and evolution. *Sustainability* of change and expansion is a natural part of effective spiritual practice. There is entry into the sustainable, unconditional loving energy field and the presence of grace.

Microdosing

Microdosing is not really covered here. The microdosing experience has no threshold. I have not done microdosing myself. From my observations, it is a similar approach to using a psychoactive mood-altering drug. Because there are no bright chemical explosions in the energy fields, I suspect there is little or no damage to the energetic organs and membranes.

Until I do a little more research, the jury is out for me on energetic effects. I would consider microdosing to be another allopathic approach that could have value. As I said elsewhere here, educating the consciousness is a superior approach that, at the least, should be combined with this type of approach to transform consciousness.

Chapter 13:
Subconscious Help or Hurt

"As a more encompassing concept, the noetic field surrounds and interpenetrates this auric energy field, embracing our multidimensionality from ego to Source." The reality of self as a conscious energy field gives us a way to approach life itself as generative and therapeutic. An understanding of these field dynamics enables us to apply the mystery of transformation. This energy, though nonphysical, appears through a gradation of attributes specific to the dimension or realm one is accessing."

Robert Waterman, EdD, *Eyes Made of Soul*

From a quantum perspective, the subconscious is an energy field surrounding and interpenetrating the physical body, aura, and energy anatomy. It's an encompassing aspect of consciousness. The subconscious provides remarkable functions to support healthy ego function and serve the evolution of consciousness.

As an **Integrating Field**, it integrates our experiences into our consciousness. The **Holding Dynamic** provides stability and sustainability to healthy ego function. The spiraling action allows us to learn, grow, and evolve. The holding dynamic filters for completion. The **Information Flow Dynamic** is an information highway between all aspects of consciousness, especially between the High Self, Basic Self, and Conscious Self.

Vital Patterns

Human consciousness has many patterns essential to life, health, and well-being. One set is the biological and energetic rhythms of living organisms. Life-sustaining rhythms such as the circadian rhythm, hormonal cycles, organ function cycles, and brain wave cycles. The heartbeat/pump pattern, based on a rhythmic electrical impulse, is essential to life. There are many such patterns.

Our aura and energy bodies also have consciousness-sustaining rhythms. There is the movement of energetic fluids between bodies and organs. There is the rhythmic opening and closing of our chakra centers as they integrate and transmute multiple energy frequencies. Healthy functioning of all our energetic rhythms and patterns are vital components to a healthy consciousness.

As a Holding Field, the subconscious is where life experiences, including behaviors, feelings, and thoughts, are held as energy patterns. Behavior patterns, habit patterns, addiction, and obsessive patterns all live as energy patterns within the subconscious. *Energetic constructs,* the holographic particles of experience/response, are held here. An energy pattern is either negative/limiting or positive/expanding.

A healthy pattern might be a positive habit such as regular exercise or a clear sense of purpose to choose a fulfilling and uplifting career aligned with our life path. A limiting pattern could be a negative habit such as tobacco addiction or heroin addiction. Or it might be a self-limiting pattern, such as extremely low self-concept. Obsessive patterns with sexuality, eating, or other normal body functions and activities are also negative pattern examples.

Western science recognizes that personality and habit patterns are held in the subconscious field. Much of psychological therapy is aimed toward accessing unconscious material to bring it to conscious awareness for transformation. Talk therapy and psychotherapy do not generally make use of quantum perspectives to transform consciousness.

Pattern Interruption Pros & Cons

I've already described the pattern interrupting dynamic that takes place in high-dose sessions. Researchers hope the dynamic of **Pattern Interruption** has therapeutic benefits. This could be great news if interrupted negative habits outweigh positive interruptions. The bad news is there is no way to control which patterns are disrupted. Healthy positive patterns and rhythms may just as easily be disrupted.

Pattern interruption has the potential to disrupt our relationship with negative dependencies, habits, and addictions. If a connection to a negative pattern is interrupted, a door opens to potentially release, replace, or clear the habit or addiction. This is a hope for researchers.

Psychotropics used this way are bound within the Newtonian approach. There are side effects. An allopathic researcher might say the disruption of a healthy pattern is a side effect. It's not. In actual practice, any pattern can be disrupted. Pattern interruption doesn't discriminate, despite a therapist or researcher's goal.

This area is where I see some of the most insidious damage caused by psychotropic drugs to the human energy field. I say insidious because identifying the cause for time-delayed psychopathology is extremely challenging to pinpoint. When a lack of motivation shows up five or ten years later, it's almost impossible to attribute a cause.

Some people have a strong consciousness and can hold, or appear to hold, a healthy response despite the interrupting action. They appear to maintain over many trips. I was part of this group. These folks are in the minority.

Other people experience disruption once and end up in a mental institution. I had a couple of friends who experienced this. They are also in the minority. Most people are in-between. Keep in mind, while I appeared to hold a healthy response, there was tremendous damage to my energy organs and membranes.

Ancient, indigenous, and aboriginal cultures have been extremely careful with psychotropic use. They recognize how essential set and setting are. They include rituals and ceremonies as an educational format to support positive outcomes. Education of consciousness is essential to any successful use of psychedelics for uplifting transformation. Even so, some shamans and guides end up side-tracked into borderline behavior.

Psychedelics directly impact the way the subconscious holds energy patterns. Psychedelic experience *does not transform* energy patterns in the field. This is one reason the ego structure returns unchanged. Rather, it disrupts the track or alignment of communication between pattern and consciousness. It disrupts our relationship with the pattern.

Disruption of Higher Guidance

Consider how information exchange within the subconscious field is patterned. The communication medium is the subconscious. Intersystem information exchange is vital for consciousness to function in healthy vibrant ways. Healthy subconscious function facilitates synchronization. Synchronization supports health and well-being energetically, psychologically, and physically.

A healthy exchange of information keeps our daily life on track and on purpose with our life path. On-purpose with our life path involves career, relationship, and any of our expressions in the physical world. It could be seen as our "spiritual path."

Balance and harmony rely on it. Inner connection, cohesion, and union result. Our experience of intuition, rightness, and purposefulness results from clear inner information exchanges.

A primary aspect of information exchange involves the three selves. The union or alignment of these is sometimes known as the Spiritual Marriage. We thrive, grow, and mature with direction from higher consciousness (Soul and High Self). Simultaneously, cooperation and support with our Basic Self provide emotional balance and maturity and gives us greater conscious access to subconscious and unconscious parts of ourselves.

Conceptualize the flow of communication between the Basic Self and Conscious Self like a train track. It may also be seen as an energy pathway through chakras between various energy membranes and bodies. High Self sends unconscious content to the Basic Self. The Basic then relays it to Conscious Self and thus into conscious awareness. This is very practical and normal and relates to a simple healthy life. It's an unconscious function that is vital.

Psychedelic use, especially repetitive use, pushes us off our subconscious track or blows out portions of it. Energy patterns, as tracks, are disrupted. This represents damage to subtle body organs and membranes. Being knocked off track is damaging to the subconscious field and has clear impacts on the individual noetic field and our consciousness.

Having portions of the track broken or disrupted creates a variety of results. Again, the conditions present within our energy anatomy express as felt-sensed psychological experiences. Damage to the subconscious field may result in feeling disconnected, spacey, or ungrounded. There may be unsettling feelings or a sense of lack of direction or purpose. There could be a strong feeling of dissociation. There could be a disharmony of thought and feeling or a loss of rhythm with oneself.

Motivation might be lost and result in listlessness or lack of caring about what happens. Life feels worthless, why bother going on? Our sense of purpose is hazy. The actual energetic connection with our life path is broken.

We flounder. We are no longer sure of ourselves, what we want to do, or what direction to take in life. Anxiety or depression may develop and, in some cases, paranoia. On occasion, it may express as a psychotic break requiring medical treatment and hospitalization.

Getting off track may open us to choosing risky behaviors. Clarity about our place in life is disrupted. We may find ourselves wanting more intense sensations in our experiences. Fulfillment seems harder to reach. Our personal sense of morality or ethics no longer guides us the way it did before. Our self-integrity takes a hit. We may move toward behaviors that were off-limits before (the "gateway" concept).

As time goes by, it's difficult to ascertain where our uneasiness, lack of coherence, or directionless feelings come from. Because of this, many who used psychedelic drugs in the past, possibly years past, are unaware that present challenges relate to previous drug use.

Disruption of subconscious patterning can also take place through the expression of any addictive pattern, such as the habitual use of alcohol or marijuana. The Basic Self's job is to maintain energy systems and patterns in the physical body, aura, and personality. When the Conscious Self chooses a repetitive pattern of drug use, the Basic Self sees this as a direction from the Conscious Self and supports the habit.

Energetically speaking, habitual use of alcohol or marijuana creates a haze of these substances in the communication line between you and your High Self. It begins to cloud awareness of your life path. It slowly clouds internal morals and ethics. This is actual damage to the energy bodies.

Habitual drug use or highly focused behavior habits could become obsessive. Obsession is a more deeply rooted pattern. Obsessions tend to move into the unconscious as well as the subconscious. The track connecting the life path and accompanying integrity and morality becomes damaged or broken. It may take a great deal of time, energy, and focus for the abuser to overcome, nullify, and retrack this habitual negative patterning.

It is especially challenging because the track for motivation and purpose is disrupted. The abuser may see a need for change, a need to break free from the obsessive habit pattern. But tackling habit breaking may appear fruitless, unreasonable, or insurmountable.

When the communication link between Basic Self and Conscious Self is disrupted, when the primary path relaying our direction and purpose is damaged, repair and reclamation is often a long-term process. I am still aware of and still struggle with damage that took place 40 years ago. My use of marijuana and psychedelics profoundly damaged my aura and subconscious field. I still struggle with motivation and memory. I still struggle with dissociation and feelings of being off-purpose.

It is difficult to focus on a spiritual path when you are traumatically disturbed psychologically and overcome by imbalance, external influence, or living in delusional or aberrant realities. It is challenging to focus on a spiritual path when feeling out of control, struggling with a lack of self-discipline, or having anxiety, depression, and addiction issues.

A holistic approach to marijuana or psychedelic use and research needs to include awareness of our energy anatomy in the concept of consciousness. The energetic human is a huge part of consciousness. The physical body is like the tip of the iceberg. Learning to see through quantum eyes is crucial to our journey over the threshold into a new worldview.

Note: The information I shared in this chapter is based on my own direct experience of habits and addictions as energy patterns in my consciousness. As I left the drug world breaking the habits in my

subconscious seemed beyond my reach. As I studied with my spiritual teacher and worked on my spiritual practice, I slowly accessed awareness of radiant energies filtering into my consciousness. These radiant energies were vital to my success in overcoming addictions and healing disconnection to my life path.

Chapter 14:
Plant Spirit Guardians

"The visible world is the invisible organization of energy."
Physicist Heinz Pagels, *The Cosmic Code*

The naturally occurring substances – THC in marijuana, mescaline in peyote, psilocybin in mushrooms, DMT in Ayahuasca and toad medicine, and LSD in ergot or seeds – all come from living plants or microorganisms. Universal-guiding intelligence becomes specific. All plants, animals, and microorganisms have an invisible guiding intelligence that implements their blueprint to grow and prosper (in a quantum world, even elements such as air, fire, earth, and water have something like this.)

Aboriginal and shamanistic traditions relate to these guiding forces as Spirit Guardians, Plant Spirits, or Plant Medicine. They are also known as Devas and Elementals. Devas are the guiding intelligence for living organisms and Elementals for the elements. Devic forms activate, support, and maintain the plant, animal, insect, and microbial kingdoms.

Most cultures have traditions and myths about Spirit Guardians or Devas. The cultures that use psychotropic substances from plants or animals always have some kind of relationship with these guiding forms. During one time period, when I worked with shamans, I had very concrete and direct experiences with the Devic kingdom.

In my own experience with magic mushrooms and peyote, when I was tripping, I became aware of the presence of the Plant Spirits present within the plant or fungus. They have a definite presence.

While the underlying consciousness of Plant Spirits is evolving, they are fully loyal to their job. That is a key aspect of their consciousness. Their job is to create, oversee, and maintain the living forms within their kingdom. Their kingdom is all life forms on the planet, so they are deeply embedded in magnetic energy frequencies.

The consciousness of Devic and elemental forms is different than human awareness. From a human perspective, their awareness is limited compared to ours. While humans evolve to greater self-awareness as spiritual beings, Spirit Guardians are set up to be absolutely loyal to their job of growing and guiding plant or animal forms or elements they are in charge of.

The Devic and elemental forms have a self-awareness that does not include free choice. Instead, their awareness has unconditional loyalty to its function within creation. Devic consciousness does not provide a bridge to self-realization, although it may advance toward human consciousness. Their innate loyalty to activate, support, and maintain aspects of creation is a central part of their governing purpose.

Through my high-dose drug experiences, I first became aware of the consciousness of Plant Spirits. When I was high on marijuana, I was under the influence of the awareness within the high. The definite ceiling where marijuana blocks access to higher spiritual frequencies also reflects the consciousness and loyalty of its Plant Spirit.

While marijuana has a ceiling that blocks access to higher-frequency *radiant energies*, it has attributes that may be soothing and healing at the level of magnetic energies. Marijuana and its cannabinoids could have effects supporting physical-level healing. The Plant Spirit oversees this communion of aiding humans in the dual magnetic levels.

When under the high-dose influence of psychedelics, the expansive and dramatic quality of the experience can easily mask the reality that the Spirit Guardian's energy frequency is very low compared to human consciousness. It doesn't mean they can't help us and teach us about things in their realm.

It has been noted, especially in shamanistic tradition, that Plant/Animal/Elemental Spirits like to interact with human consciousness. Human consciousness shows them a huge leap in awareness. While they teach us about their realm, they also learn from us, so they promote our continuing communion with them in their world.

I noticed that, when I engaged the consciousness of a Plant Spirit within a high or trip, I joined its *lens of perception* and entered its awareness field. The Plant Spirit naturally embraces me with its level of awareness. This embrace is like an umbrella. I'm in its domain and align with its loyalties. By taking the drug, I consent to open myself to Plant Spirit influences. I give over some level of my own inner authority to it.

Plant medicine certainly opens us up to greater psychic awareness, no question about that. I am talking about the difference between psychic levels and spiritual levels, magnetic realms, and spiritual realms. In my experience, engaging the psychic realms asks for more karma. Psychic realms are deeply embedded in cause and effect. Drugs do not bring release from magnetic karma. They tend to pull us in more deeply.

Keep in mind that we can engage Devas without the use of drugs. There is a healthy communion between humans and Devas that is very expansive. Growing food is one example of this.

Plant-based formulas used as healing medicine is another example. We use non-psychoactive herbal remedies to bring about healthy positive changes in our bodies, minds, and emotions. In fact, herbology works amazingly well in healing and supporting our energy bodies and organs.

Many indigenous and aboriginal peoples have long-standing relationships with nature spirits within their culture and way of life. These nature spirits may assist them in many ways. In my perception, especially when survival is at stake, having nature spirits on your side and working with you makes a solid positive difference in how you live and grow.

Psychedelic use sets up a different scenario. We typically go to their level. Seeing life through the awareness of a Plant Spirit is altered and very different. We can be inspired to think this is amazing and profound. Yet our human multidimensional consciousness is far more expansive than Devic and Elemental consciousness.

With marijuana plant derivatives such as CBD, CBG, CBC, and others, which are said to be non-psychoactive, for me, the jury is still out. In my observation, CBD is psychoactive, though mildly so. I am aware the marijuana Plant Spirit Guardian has a long history with human beings. How the Plant Spirit of marijuana affects human consciousness through derivatives like CBD is a question for me. Be a spiritual scientist and observe all the effects. If CBD is being used as another suppression-based chemical, it must be closely observed in the long run.

Chapter 15:
Which Drug?

"During this time, your system stops its normal pattern and moves off its customary path. You go up real high, and when you're up, because of the abnormally rapid acceleration rate, you reach into a "higher consciousness." You do; there's no question about that at all. But when you come back down, you have to enter into a compensatory pattern; you have to balance the action."

John-Roger DSS, *Spiritual High*

This chapter is related to my experiences doing Noetic Balancing. Around ten years into my training and practice of Noetic Balancing my ability to perceive energetically became keen enough to notice more subtle energetic presence and effects in the human energy field. My sharing of energetic qualities and effects is based on that.

Stimulants

Stimulants and cocaine have dramatic effects on the energy field. I had clients who were speed freaks or cocaine junkies in the past. Energy field effects from these are similar to the effects of psychedelic drugs like LSD, DMT, or mescaline. There may be tearing and shredding of bodies, organs, and membranes in the energy field. Long-term methamphetamine or cocaine addiction may become an obsession.

CBD

CBD, in my perception, has very subtle or minimal psychoactive effects on consciousness. Also, note a CBD product may state "THC-free" when it contains trace amounts. Hemp-derived cannabinoids like CBD, which are not overtly psychoactive, likely end up on the health food store shelves sold like any herbal remedy.

CBD and other marijuana alkaloids, when the whole plant is used recreationally, act to modulate THC's effect on consciousness. CBD moderates the euphoric effect. It plays an active part in affecting neurochemistry and has a part in affecting our moods.

When my dad was in the final stages of life, a family member wanted to give him CBD to help with his pain. None of us really wanted to use opioids. My dad was hypersensitive to them.

CBD ended up overstimulating him. Various dosages and mixtures with THC, prescribed by a doctor, were tried, and they all produced the same effect. They did not appear to relieve pain but rather wound him up to the degree it didn't work for him. So, we took him off the CBD.

I found it interesting how pharmaceutical suggestions for CBD, as to effect, were such that three different products with varying amounts of CBD only, or CBD with varying amounts of THC, could be prescribed for pain or prescribed to stimulate or sedate. Any one of the products could be prescribed for any of the three symptoms. Interesting.

I looked at this and realized that, since marijuana was legalized, the use and effects of CBD are in a highly experimental phase and being prescribed through trial and error. Like pretty much all psychoactive drugs, researchers do not actually know how effects in consciousness take place. They can observe cannabinoids going into receptor sites but don't really understand how resulting changes manifest in consciousness.

Among various friends who tried CBD for general conditions, I get a variety of reports. Some use a tincture or salve and said they think, *maybe*, they are getting a positive effect. Others said certain aches and pains diminished. Other friends taking CBD orally in some form or another, in various doses, report increased energy, which seems to be what I hear most often. The only miracle cures I hear about are in advertising by those who sell the products.

Friends who take products with CBD that include THC usually report some change in consciousness. Often, they use these products for mood alteration as a way to deal with stress or anxiety. Some said their moods are lifted with a little THC included with the CBD. In my observations of folks taking CBD-THC combinations, the THC has all the same effects as I previously mentioned.

Even though CBD is only mildly psychoactive, for some, CBD blocks the connection to higher-frequency *radiant energies*. This especially applies if you are a Sound Current initiate or have a spiritual practice where you regularly connect with higher-frequency *radiant energies*. The marijuana Plant Spirit may be involved in this.

Tobacco

Regular tobacco users have a thin, dry, brittle shell of energy surrounding the physical body, usually within two or three inches from the skin. The length of use and amount are reflected in the strength of this shell. The way a long-time user's skin gets dry and wrinkly is a manifestation of this energetic shell. It probably also relates to the constriction of blood vessels.

In my experience, when I'm doing a physical Noetic Balancing with a person, this 'shell' diminishes but does not completely clear. One balancing will not clear this shell. Energetically, the shell is both the tobacco frequency of energy and the manifestation of changes to energy and biology by long-term tobacco use. The clearing of this shell only takes place over time after the person has stopped using tobacco. This shell does not appear to impede the clearing of blocks in the energy field directly.

A habitual tobacco user typically has two primary responses to use. The first is the inhibiting and deadening of the emotional body. This is the reaction of users who smoke to deal with stressful situations and anxiety. As time goes by, this energetic function seems to strengthen. That is, a habitual smoker gets greater emotional relief by smoking tobacco than a novice smoker. The perceived shell in the auric field relates to this emotional deadening.

The shell blocks the skin's pranic energy, causing it to lose resilience and flexibility and get dry and wrinkly. Tobacco smoke also blocks the flow of prana into the lungs from the air that is breathed (and damages the lungs).

Tobacco, like marijuana, also blocks the inflow of higher-frequency energy or light through the crown and brow chakras, though in a minor way. Any substance blocking the emotions or creating a stasis in the causal body also interferes with the flow of higher-frequency energy, light, or *radiant energies* into the body.

We have observed blocking and suppressing energy flow in our energetic anatomy eventually causes illness. The stagnant energy promotes disease. One could say the quality of suppression is carcinogenic.

The second response is that tobacco users typically have a robust subconscious pattern or dependency, which is a separate issue from the presence of the substance in the aura. This energy pattern or dependency does not seem to have any direct dramatic effect on the Life-Pattern for most people.

As Balancers, we are not too concerned with the presence of tobacco in the aura, though the issues or challenges which lead to the forming of a dependency may come up to be cleared and resolved. Any strong addictive pattern in the subconscious will, at some point, delay spiritual progression. Initiates to the Sound Current must clear these habitual patterns to progress spiritually. As we evolve in spiritual awareness, addiction patterns in the subconscious and Etheric Body *must* be released and cleared to advance.

Alcohol

Long-term drinking, including binge drinking and functioning alcoholism, has the same effect on the subconscious track as previously discussed. This is a primary energetic effect. It may have a big impact on the health and functionality of the consciousness. The auras of committed drinkers reflect longer-term effects that must be cleared, and these may reflect physical damage to the body.

Alcohol residue tends to clear from the energy field relatively quickly. A drink or two on Friday is usually clear by Monday or so. This is the opposite of a marijuana high, which typically lingers in the energy field for a month or two, or more.

Consistent alcohol use, as it damages organic organs and membranes, also damages the membranes in the energy field. Again, a holographic view is multi-directional. We could always think about this by the reality that physical body effects always correlate and reflect in the energy field. Alcohol is extremely hard on physical organs and tissues when taken in excess.

Alcohol users do *not* have a "snowstorm" or static energy field in their aura as marijuana users do. It just doesn't do the same thing. Alcohol frequency and marijuana/psychedelic frequencies are quite different. With alcohol, the greater effect appears to be caused by biochemical effects that become energetic effects.

Addictive and obsessive alcohol use causes tears in the energy field membranes in similar ways and locations as marijuana and other psychotropic drugs. Strong addictive or obsessive patterns in the consciousness do this regardless of the focus. Sometimes, alcohol use and alcohol dependency open the aura to outside psychic influence.

Since alcohol use is pretty much always recreational, when we drink, we also give over authority to a substance. Our conscious choice to relinquish authority, getting tipsy or drunk, opens the door to certain outside influences, such as psychic entities, which may enter into our field via psychic frequencies of energy.

During a Noetic Balancing, alcohol residue from recent drinking is readily cleared as the process progresses. Longer-term effects in the aura can also be cleared and repaired, supporting the healing of organic damage as time goes by. While alcohol in the aura may present as a deadening, it could also show up in terms of the issues around which committed drinking takes place. Those are the issues we want to avoid or forget by drinking.

Prescription Drugs

Our healthcare culture has become very drug oriented. We are a pill-popping culture. Most prescription drugs leave little perceivable residue in the energy field. Typically, they don't need to be addressed in a balancing session. They are energetically clear (this does not imply they do not have side effects or may *not* be the best choice for a person).

In Noetic Balancing work, I encounter and am aware of many of the anti-depressant or anti-anxiety drugs currently in use. They are not obvious energetically and require a fine-tuned awareness to spot. Benzodiazepines or Prozac, for example. I notice they have a *similar* effect in the energy field to marijuana/THC.

They primarily affect the emotional/causal level. I perceive a stasis or neutralizing effect in the emotional level of the energy field. Effects from these types of prescription drugs are not as dramatic or prevalent as THC. They do not get in the way of balancing work and do not show up as "damage" to the energy field.

When a prescription drug like Benzodiazepine is used long-term and creates a physical dependency, there may also be an addictive pattern in the subconscious. Only in more severe cases do I see the addiction pattern block progression in consciousness.

If the person also educates their consciousness by seeing a counselor or doing effective self-growth and educational work, they generally expand and mature past the onset issue – anxiety or depression, let's say – and naturally go off of the prescription drug over time.

With any mood modification drugs used to combat anxiety, or depression, or promote sleep, their primary mechanism suppresses, blocks, or causes separation of some kind in one or more of our levels, primarily emotional. That's what they are prescribed to do. They are designed to create a buffer between our feelings and our conscious awareness.

This is an allopathic approach. Treating symptoms has its place. Yet, we need to expand our understanding of the practice. I'm not sure why suppression has become a primary course of treatment. As a trained counselor I was taught that educating consciousness (therapy) was the most effective way to bring transformation.

A more whole perspective of human consciousness is needed. Feelings are information serving a purpose. It is helpful to understand they may reveal unresolved issues and thus have an underlying purpose toward completion and integration. They guide and support us into expansion, growth, maturation, and evolution.

If we don't do consciousness work to clear the underlying cause, the medication may stop working or side effects could become more severe. Suppression wasn't meant to be used long-term. Consciousness may move to get attention with more abrupt or severe eruptions emotionally. Disconnecting from our emotional body masks awareness. The bottom line is we must find what works to expand awareness rather than suppress awareness.

Pain Relievers

Pain medication and opiates deaden nerve receptivity. This deadening of the nervous system shows up in the aura as blank or soft fuzzy areas in the field. This deadening of the nervous system (and specific brain function) reflects a deadening of consciousness in general. It slows down energy movement in the field and impairs the functionality of energy organs.

Opiate and painkiller dependencies block a person from their emotional issues. Opioids suppress and numb the emotional body. While the purpose of taking pain medications is to lower physical discomfort, the accompanying euphoria and overall deadening promote psychological dependency (there may also be a physical dependency). The euphoria is sensation-based and masks emotional distress or imbalance.

Generational addictive hereditary patterns in one of the bodies may appear as archetypes at the etheric or unconscious level. There may be a genetic miasma, which is a predisposition. Addiction patterns may be instituted as part of the life path to work through a learning opportunity.

A physical-level balancing could clear much of the drug's effect rather rapidly (sometimes to the client's dismay). The emotional and mental/spiritual level balancing may help clear underlying patterns leading to the desire to deaden the consciousness.

In my observation, the current opioid "crisis" reflects deeper self-worth, motivation, and purposefulness issues for many people. There is a call for us to connect more fully with meaning and purpose in our lives. Numbing or deadening ourselves is a symptom of larger cultural issues. Our cultural training falls short in teaching emotional intelligence and life skills.

The closed-ended Newtonian worldview supporting suppression is unwittingly promoting deeper anguish, loss, and disconnection rather than supporting health, expansion, and well-being.

PART IV:
TRANSCENDENCE

"Awakening is a very active process through which step-by-step you remove or dissolve the barriers from your consciousness that are all that prevent you from knowing your Soul's nature— from experientially knowing that you are the Presence of Love."

Mary R. Hulnick, Ph.D., H. Ronald Hulnick, Ph.D., *Remembering the Light Within.*

Chapter 16:
Revelations of Transcendence

We are holographic beings. The pathways of cause and effect within our consciousness are multi-directional. We are an energetic coalescence. The biology of our physical body is simply one pathway, one facet of who we are as multidimensional beings. The states of our energy bodies/fields, our biochemistry, and our psychological experiences are correlated. Our biological selves and spiritual/energetic selves are reflective correlates.

Winston Hampton

Transcendence seems like it has a charge on it to describe something magical, wonderful, and only remotely attainable. As I share here, I suppose I pretty much ignore all that. This chapter is based on my own experiences. I found many definitions out there to be insufficient, so I base my definition on my experience.

What We Call Transcendence

Many who experienced spontaneous transcendence say it's beyond mental explanation. Others don't want to talk about it in the abstract. Transcendence is especially challenging to research through a Newtonian *lens of perception*. Modern western science excludes the very elements that precipitate it. Invisible Spirit, the Authentic Self, and accompanying *radiant energies* are the bedrock of transcendence.

In chapter four I gave a brief personal definition of transcendence as a dynamic of high-dose experience. I said it is an altered state of consciousness taking us beyond normal ego limitations and defenses. It may include experiences of invisible spiritual realms accompanied by mystical realization.

I also said there is a presence of mystical ecstasy or bliss. The value of transcendence is positive uplifting change bringing greater balance, health, and loving with deeper purpose and understanding. Life issues somehow resolve and the positive change is sustainable.

My exploration of life has been guided by my desire for direct experience. This is not an intellectual discussion about transcendence in the abstract. Rather, it is a look through the eyes of direct experience revealing revelations outside the box. My spiritual teacher taught me to approach spiritual advancement practically. The lens of a spiritual scientist does nicely.

A spiritual scientist lens takes transcendence and anchors it into the living reality of, "This is my experience now. Is it working for me or not?" Understanding is based on direct experience. I simply observe my present ongoing experiences and behaviors to see what works for me and what does not.

Attaining higher levels of human consciousness seems to be inferred from how we see transcendence. Spiritual scientists have the intention to do just that. How do I self-actualize in the highest way? We bring change to the world by changing ourselves first. In our reach for transcendence, we ask:

- Am I experiencing more joy in my life?
- Am I transcending my addictions, fears, and anxieties?
- Am I at peace with myself?
- Am I able to love unconditionally?
- Can I observe reality with caring neutrality?
- Am I on purpose and enthusiastic with my life?

When it comes to using psychotropics as entheogens, as a means to spiritual transcendence, these are questions we must ask ourselves.

I come to the meaning for transcendence backward. Instead of defining it and then trying to substantiate the definition, I have the experience first, then observe what is present. Therefore, transcendent experience, including what sustains, may include:

- Unity or all-is-one consciousness
- An experience of timelessness
- Interconnected experiences
- Infinite possibilities
- Potent creativity
- Flexibility and resilience

- Unconditional love and caring
- Joy, enthusiasm, and fulfillment

For those of us seeking transcendence, we hope for experiences that are uplifting and expansive, supporting the highest and best qualities of a fulfilling life. We seek to transcend and transform limiting qualities such as low self-esteem, negative self-judgment, anxiety, or fear. We hope for greater self-empowerment and success grounded in confidence, purpose, loving, strength, caring, understanding, and wisdom. We hope to come away with a new understanding about ourselves and life leading to sustainable fulfillment.

Spontaneous Transcendence

Back to my question in chapter 11: Is there a difference between Psychotropic Transcendence and natural or Spontaneous Transcendence? Yes, there is a difference. Hidden within the possible life-changing, mystical threshold experience is a world of difference. Let's advance to a quantum view.

Either psychotropic or spontaneous transcendence offers us life-changing Reference Points. Both provide a peek into altered states of consciousness diametrically different from our 'normal' state of consciousness. Both bring us over a threshold and bypass egoic limitations. Both give us a brief direct experience of life that may include unity consciousness, timelessness, and noetic awareness of a greater Divine intelligence.

If both bring this experience, then what's the difference between them? The answer seems simple, but as we explore it, we find multidirectional layers of complexity. Consciousness is multidirectional and multidimensional. **Spontaneous Transcendence takes place when *radiant energies* flow into us, either from Universal Source or from Soul.** Spontaneous Transcendence is precipitated by the presence and inflow of *radiant energies* in an individual's consciousness.

I talked about my perception of *radiant energies* already. Given they are the essential element of spontaneous transcendence, let's explore them in more depth. Sufi poet Rumi said, *"Out beyond ideas of wrongdoing and right-doing, there is a field. I'll meet you there."* The field he talks about is a state of consciousness or an energy field beyond yin/yang, right/wrong, beginning and end.

Radiant energies are singular spiritual energy fields or forms originating beyond the polar/dual field of creation. They might be perceived as energy fields or energy frequencies, but they are also states of consciousness. When one experiences unity consciousness, it is not "out there". The experiencer *is* unity consciousness along with everything else.

One of my consciousness teachers said something like, "We are not humans with a Soul, we are Souls having a human experience." Authentic Self or Soul is the energy source or life-source enlivening who we are. As such, as energy, it transcends duality. In essence, we are Soul, our bodies and ego personality are clothing the Soul wears.

Soul is a holographic particle of the original Divine Source. Soul as energy is a *radiant energy* that is singular, beyond dual form. As human beings, the presence of Soul in us, as us, is the first *radiant energy*. Because our true self is Soul, we are able to receive, attune to, and experience universal *radiant energies*.

What I call *radiant energies* are well known and observed. Most religions and spiritual traditions, along with quantum physics, acknowledge and portray the presence of *radiant energies*. As a spiritual scientist, I observe them with no religious affiliation. In essence, they transcend any possible belief system formed about them. They transcend the mental dimension which is based on duality. The mental concept or any name for them is a symbol for them.

We labeled them as best we could for identification and conversation. In various religions, they have been called Holy Spirit, Christ Consciousness, Spirit of God, the Void, Nothingness, the Light, Cosmic Light, and Celestial Lights.

Radiant energies are also known as Sound. The Word, the Sound Current, Shabd, Dhun, Vadan, Anahad, the Audible Life Stream, Celestial Melodies, and Saute Surmadi are references to *radiant energies* as sound.

Many folks, myself included, recognize the direct experience of these *radiant energies*. We perceive these energies universally and neutrally. In their presence, although they are invisible, beyond the light spectrum, a glow may be seen. When I "see" their presence, I see with the eyes of Soul, not my physical eyes. Spiritual traditions and religions depict their presence as halos or radiance around people.

What causes *radiant energies* to be present with a person precipitating Spontaneous Transcendence? Consciousness is incredibly complex. Each of us has a Life Path and an evolutionary history as individual beings. We are wholly embedded within Universal Intelligence. A primary characteristic of *radiant energy* is original intelligence, not the mind. It's what guides and directs all unfolding reality.

Our Soul in union, collaboration, and agreement with Original Living Intelligence carries out the day-to-day process of life. Soul is original intelligence, and the guidance and wisdom of universal intelligence are also outside the Soul. What this all boils down to is *radiant energies* know, guide and precipitate in perfect timing for the advent of a Spontaneous Transcendent experience.

The precipitating presence of *radiant energies* is wholly in alignment with what's next, what's best, and what fulfills all aspects of the needs of each person. The ego has no say in this. The conscious awareness for most of us has little say.

The ego personality is deeply limited. The knowing and guidance of *radiant energies* are infinite and all-encompassing. This knowing is incomprehensible and inaccessible to the intellect or mind.

As *radiant energies* flow or manifest into consciousness they "ride" magnetic energies that are present. They seem to concentrate at the crown and brow chakras as they appear. Our magnetic energy systems provide a network of passage. Keep in mind that all our bodies, biology, and energy anatomy are made of magnetic frequencies.

In the physical body, they move upon the neural and vascular networks. They are a version of consciousness, which affects and is affected on all physical, emotional, and mental levels. This radiant "Light" has innate qualities to enhance alignment, balance, awakening, transformation, and healing any part our whole consciousness system. I have come to see this innate quality of goodness, the flow of *radiant energies,* as unconditional loving.

This "Light" penetrates our very cells. *Radiant energies* elicit biochemical cascades throughout the physical body. The endocrine system, hormonal system, brain, neurotransmitters, and nervous system are all prompted. This biochemical prompting has systemic effects.

Part of the transcendent experience is now biological. Our biology, obviously an integral part of the experience, enhances and expands our experience in various ways. Biological level healing may take place, spontaneously or over time.

Biochemical cascades are knowingly guided to initiate change in the physical body. Systems in the body get a frequency upgrade increasing their ability to hold, sustain, and transmit higher frequencies of light. Adjustments are made to clear imbalances or illnesses present now or later.

Neurotransmitters are adjusted to provide biological experiences to align and enhance higher experiences of joy, fulfillment, on-purposefulness, worthiness, and loving. Our evolution of spiritual awakening is a holistic process involving all our bodies.

We awaken spiritually, which has little to do with this physical level. Spontaneous Transcendence knows how to guide this. Still, our evolution also expresses and fulfills through our physical body in our imagination, emotions, mind, and unconscious. Our physical, emotional, mental, and unconscious states are an integral part of our movement into spiritual awakening!

After I quit using drugs and met my spiritual teacher and consciousness teachers, I became aware these higher frequencies of energy were working with me. In my experience, in cooperation with my efforts to heal and expand, they dissolved the addiction patterns in my subconscious. They gave me an etheric body overlay to contain and protect me energetically and to support my healing on various levels. They worked steadily with me over some years and still do now.

I experienced the Higher Powers that know what and how to do things I did not know how to do. Not only did I receive healing and balancing in the presence of these *radiant energies*, but I also was blessed with ongoing experiences of Spontaneous Transcendence. I diligently applied myself to my spiritual practice but learned over time it was the *radiant energies* that precipitated and guided my mystical or transcendental experiences.

Spiritual awakening and transcendental expansion align with the Highest Good. It's a natural movement of *radiant energies* unfolding out of the Universal Noetic Field's intelligence in conjunction and agreement with the Soul and High Self. The *radiant energies* manifest as joy, loving, balancing, releasing, comforting, and clearing. They bring qualities informing the individual consciousness in ways that heal, harmonize, unify and awaken. Further, they educate, inform, and evolve the ego and Basic Self.

Psychotropic Transcendence

Human biochemistry is integral to the transcendental experience. Consciousness is multidirectional and includes input from all our bodies – physical, imaginal, emotional, mental, and unconscious. Psychotropics are a chemical key affecting biochemistry. Their unique chemical makeup causes biochemical changes similar to those taking place during Spontaneous

Transcendent experiences. Psychedelic effects on biochemistry *mimic* radiant energy elicited biochemical cascades.

Psychedelics are a shortcut to altered states of consciousness. There is clearly some value in this. They provide direct experience to altered states through Ego Bypass. They can bring deeply mystical or spiritual experiences. Reference Points may be found offering the possibility of a more fulfilling experience of life. Pattern Interruption could offer therapeutic value.

Current research and focus about psychedelics and their effects on consciousness are being done within the Newtonian paradigm, which doesn't recognize the full multidimensionality of human consciousness. Human energetic anatomy is excluded to a great degree. The invisible *radiant energies* absolutely essential to who we are and our health, vitality, and evolution, are invisible to Newtonian eyes.

Lacking awareness of *radiant energies*, the biochemical cascades taking place during transcendence are seen as a cause rather than an effect. This is a huge miss. Biochemical reactions set in motion by substances such as LSD, ayahuasca, peyote, or mushrooms don't result in anything like what takes place in the presence of *radiant energies*. Transcendence resulting from a psychopharmacological approach to opening our energy bodies is based, at least to some degree, on damage taking place in energy bodies, membranes, and organs.

In my experience with drug-induced transcendence, I had mind expansions and spiritual realizations almost identical to Spontaneous Transcendence. The *almost* is actually a vast area. It is subtle and challenging to verbalize, but the *absence* of a wise, loving presence that is overseeing and guiding the process is very different. The Light-filled nuances of Spontaneous Transcendence are missing. The basic experience is there but there is a sharpness and harshness present in the drug-induced state.

It's like walking along a trail that is slippery and icy with patches of dense fog and pouring rain. There is a one-thousand-foot drop on both sides. It's hard to see and challenging to keep a solid footing. That's walking the path with a drug.

Conversely, there's another where you walk along the trail in bright sunlight. It winds through meadows filled with wildflowers. It's dry and even, and the footing is clear and solid.

Both trails reach destinations that are worth hiking to.

Change and transformation taking place through Spontaneous Transcendence are healthy and sustainable as well as subtle. *Radiant energies* guide the process. Drug-induced transcendence has no such guidance and does not sustain.

We wouldn't want transcendence elicited this way to be sustainable. At the session's high point, the ego structure is forced to change and is not prepared to maintain this level of perception.

Eventually, an ongoing, drug-induced peak would result in a psychotic break.

Perhaps psychotropic substances, which originate in plants, animals, or fungi, are meant to be used by humans to access altered states of consciousness. Possibly, quick access is needed to help push human evolution along. In my experience, when a psychotropic is used in a high-dose setting, enlightened revealing realizations can occur. If the user does this once or twice and then moves on, damage to the energy bodies is slight. The Reference Points may be worthwhile.

If you use psychedelics as a shortcut it's vital to know all the ramifications. Past psychedelic users who I have worked with in Noetic Balancing all had some level of damage to their consciousness, within their energy anatomy. In Newtonian parlance, the damage is side effects. Do the side effects we incur outweigh the value? Ask the spiritual scientist questions. Have I expanded into greater joy, peace, loving, and fulfillment? Is the value sustaining?

Our world is in deep need of a global paradigm shift in human consciousness in how we see, live, and treat ourselves and our world. We must expand beyond Newtonian philosophy. We must add the quantum/spiritual findings of an energetic world to our view and approach to research and life.

Further research on psychedelics as entheogens or for therapy must be done holistically. Our energy anatomy must be included.

We must expand our awareness of who we are as spiritual beings having a human experience.

PART V:

HEALING, REGENERATION, AND UPLIFTMENT

"Energy follows thought. That means if you are thinking about a hot fudge sundae, all the levels of your consciousness come in line to bring that to you. The same is true for envisioning and moving toward higher awareness and Soul transcendence. All of your levels will start making that happen. You will receive cooperation from your mind, emotions, basic selves; even your subconscious will be guiding you though you will not be consciously aware of that level. That's why it becomes so important to watch your thoughts because you will create in a physical way those things you have focused on in your thinking. Also, be careful what you say. Listen to what you say and be sure it represents what you really want in your life."

John-Roger, DSS

If you've been a drug user, for any reason, it's helpful to know how to balance and heal any after-effects you might deal with. Following my years of drug use, I spent around ten years actively catching up and coming to terms with these. The help I received and the methods I used were necessary for my next steps. My time of healing, balancing, and maturing was crucial to living a normal healthy life while continuing along my spiritual journey.

This section addresses healing and repairing damage to our energy anatomy through several approaches. Damage to energy organs and membranes shows up as psychological issues. There are various ways to approach healing or resolving psychological issues.

The way I see it, it's effective to directly address repairing and regenerating our auric fields and energy anatomy when they are damaged or out of balance. I look at three approaches to this: Psychological, energetic, and spiritual. As always, the focus is on finding what works personally for you.

Those dealing with drug addiction may want guidance and support from professionals trained in rehabilitation as a first step. Any therapeutic approach is more effective if it includes the whole person (holistic). Education and support systems are crucial.

If you are considering using psychotropics in your rehabilitation work, be informed and find practitioners with an elevated level of holistic awareness with a track record of demonstration and long-term positive results.

Personally, I'm not clear that psychotropics provide viable, safe methods for healing and curing for reasons I've already stated. I believe research needs to be done from a more holistic *lens of perception* including an in-depth examination of long-term, human energy field effects.

Chapter 17:
Psychological Approach to Healing

"When we speak of the highest good, we speak of the highest God form, the God of all things. And when you honestly ask for things "for my highest good," your experiences will be for your highest good. If you find yourself being blocked in your pursuit of a particular goal, you might be wise to step back, take another look at your actions and motivations, and reevaluate whether the goal is for your highest good and the highest good of those around you."

John-Roger, DSS

Engaging in counseling, therapy, or self-growth training is educational. In psychological parlance, it's called Cognitive Behavioral Therapy or education (CBT). When education takes place, consciousness changes and transformation takes place. The educational nature of psychological work is amazingly effective for healing on all levels.

A psychological approach might include counseling, talk therapy, dyads, triads, group work, and such. Within each school of thought are specific methods such as role-play, sandbox, self-forgiveness, affirmations, cathartic release, reflective communication, listening, empathy, gestalt, positive self-regard, art therapy, and a whole slew of psycho-dynamic techniques.

Traditional psychology generally excludes the Authentic Self. Therapy is aimed at balancing, educating, and healing the ego structure. Traditional psychology doesn't address challenges from an energetic perspective. That's okay, it works. A psychological approach is all about ego work. As I mentioned previously, ego work is key for advancing on a spiritual path or a path of self-actualization.

Still, at the crux of transformation and healing are *radiant energies*. Even if mainstream psychology excludes the Authentic Self and *radiant energies* in their theory, the reality of our energetic selves is still fully present and operating. This highlights the reality that we don't need to be consciously aware of human energetics for healing and expansion to still take place.

Spiritual Psychology includes the Authentic Self and recognizes the energetic or spiritual human being. In Spiritual Psychology, the intention for healing and expanding is based on awakening, accessing, and freeing our Authentic Selves. Awakening to our Authentic Self naturally and gracefully informs our ego work. It begins to bring balance, completion and healing to wherever it's needed within our consciousness.

Chapter 18:
Energetic Approach to Healing

"The body is a self-healing organism, so it's really about clearing things out of the way so the body can heal itself. I can tell you that anything that happens in the physical body will happen in the pattern of the energy fields first. The whole universe appears as a dynamic web of inseparable energy patterns ..."

Barbara Brennan

The Chinese developed a form of energy medicine we call acupuncture. This is a complex, holistic, medicinal process involving diagnosis and treatment. A physician of Chinese medicine wants to know much more than just your physical symptom. Their responsibility was to keep you healthy rather than treat an illness.

Traditional Chinese medicine is a health-based system. The physician would ask what you ate, your elimination process, how hard you worked, how you spent your time, what you were thinking about, and your family conditions. If your imbalances developed into a physical illness, the physician might not be paid as he failed to do his job.

Acupuncture and herbal medicine go together. In Chinese medicine, herbology is primarily energetically based, rather than the Western approach, which is biochemical. Acupuncture utilizes the meridian system.

We now know meridians are microscopic physical structures that create a vital link between the subtle and physical bodies like Nadis are in East Indian traditional Ayurvedic medicine. Chinese traditions address energy body imbalances through the meridians, which then reflect into the physical body.

Energy or Vibrational Medicine modalities are an excellent way to directly address energy field imbalances resulting from psychotropic drug use. Chinese and East Indian medicine are excellent ways to repair damage to the human energy field. Even though imbalances show up as mild to severe psychological issues ranging from depression to hallucinations, these ancient forms of assistance help heal.

There are modern energy medicine modalities with similar traits. Reiki, Polarity Balancing, Bio-energetic Bodywork, Emotional Freedom Technique (EFT), Core Energetics, Feinberg Technique, and others are also useful. Find what works for you.

Some modalities directly perceive the human energy field, observe what is there, then use techniques to effect change. The ones I'm most aware of are Noetic Balancing, Barbara Brennan's "Full Spectrum Healing," and Pranic Healing. I'm sure there are many I'm not aware of. They may use higher sense or clairvoyance to view the aura. Each has developed ways to work in the human energy field to facilitate healing and balancing.

As I mentioned earlier, I was introduced to Noetic Balancing at the Quimby Center* in the late 1970s. During the 1960s, folks would go there, or to the places they traveled, to work with Neva Dell Hunter, John Clark McDougall, Ellavivian Power, and Robert Waterman. Aura Balancing, also known as Noetic Field Therapy (NFT), and Noetic Balancing teaches how transformation is affected in the human energy field, which then transforms the psychological conditions in consciousness and heals at the physical level.

This approach, in my experience, is very effective for human energetics as it includes engaging the *radiant spiritual* and magnetic energies. The spiritual organization Movement of Spiritual Inner Awareness (MSIA) does Aura Balancing. Its founder, John-Roger, learned it from Neva Dell Hunter and Ellavivian Power, and it remains true to its original form. Noetic Balancing and MSIA's Aura Balancing are effective modalities for healing consciousness and the energy fields.

*Quimby Center was founded by Neva Dell Hunter, the center is based on Phineas Parkhurst Quimby's work in the 1800s. He is considered the father of the New Thought Movement, which is the basis for the Unity Church, Church of Religious Science, Divine Science Church, and all New Thought Movement organizations.

Noetic Balancing has a basic format. The client lies on a massage table fully clothed and face-up. The practitioner uses a pendulum in the client's aura to increase sensitivity and more subtly connect with human and spiritual energy fields. Balancing typically takes an hour to 90 minutes.

Noetic Balancing is divided into three parts. First, the physical aura is balanced, then the emotional, then the Mental/Spiritual. Some balancers, like those in MSIA, do three separate sessions to complete the levels. Regardless of whether the balancing work is one or three sessions, it may be necessary to do separate balances if there is a lot of damage to the energy field. When I balance someone with marijuana residue in the aura, it typically takes a full hour to clear it. The energy field must be cleared before any work is done on other levels.

In my opinion, many energy medicine practitioners don't seem to effect demonstrable change. When it comes to energy medicine, I prefer a results-based approach. I like to see demonstrable change take place.

As you select a practitioner, keep in mind that repair and healing take time. This is not allopathic medicine aiming to eliminate symptoms as quickly as possible. Vibrational medicine often requires patience and treatment over time. Be a *spiritual scientist* and track conditions and specific results to watch for actual demonstrable change.

Following my decade of drug use, I utilized a variety of healing methods, like Noetic Balancing. These were huge jumpstarts in my healing process. I also engaged in lots of ego work through private counseling, workshops, and personal growth training. These were all essential to my healing.

When it comes to an energetic approach to healing, there are many options available. Look for a practitioner with a holistic level of awareness and a loving-centered practice. Don't simply focus on psychic ability-centered methods. Be a *spiritual scientist*. Take a results-based approach. Be pragmatic and practical and engage in the work to get the desired results.

Chapter 19:
Spiritual Approach to Healing

"The convergence of Spirit inside of you and the alignment of your energies to God is vitally, vitally important things. We do convergence and alignment through harmonic vibrations, we do it through visualization, we do it through seeing the Light, we do it through seeing the beauty, the peace. We do it through living the best way we can, and we live it mostly by forgiving every action we've done, even this last one."

John-Roger, DSS

What makes an approach to healing spiritual? A method that consciously intends to engage *radiant energies* is considered spiritual. Effective methods of promoting and engaging them require we actively practice them. You must do them to get the value! I mention three primary methods here: visualization, chanting, and meditation.

Any spiritual methodology or approach that works, naturally and automatically begins to repair a damaged energy field. When working toward healing and balancing, it isn't necessary to discern any difference between magnetic/psychic/dual and spiritual/singular energies. As we engage spiritual methodologies, the two energy forms, magnetic and spiritual, naturally interconnect and combine. *Radiant energy* forms utilize magnetic energies.

Our physical body, emotions, and mind are magnetic energy frequencies so, obviously, when we actively practice a method, such as chanting or meditation, we engage and direct magnetic energies. Healers of any kind consciously utilize and direct magnetic frequencies in their work. Although magnetic energies may be directed, *radiant energies* are beyond direction. They direct themselves within the Highest Good.

In a spiritual approach, engagement includes our inner source. We use conscious awareness to direct. As we engage a method, we set up a format to invite *radiant energies* to come in. Higher-frequency *radiant energies* work with us through our permission and are responsive to our requests. Prayer or invocation is a conscious invitation for the presence and guidance of spiritual *radiant energies*. We want any visualization, chanting, or meditation to be within the Highest Good.

As we engage in a spiritual method or practice, we act as our own practitioners. Even when we are working with a guide or following someone, we are still responsible for the practice inside ourselves. I find it helpful and uplifting to work with consciousness teachers skilled in specific areas to help me deal with certain challenges. A consciousness teacher could be a counselor, coach, or shaman, for example.

A spiritual teacher provides a much higher level of assistance. A hallmark sign of such a teacher, in my experience, is they work in and from the invisible realms, anytime and anywhere. They are not bound by time, space, or condition in providing teaching and guidance. Spiritual teachers capable of this assist in effecting change by connecting to higher frequencies of *radiant energy* in line with the Highest Good. Thus, teaching and healing occur even when we're sleeping.

Intention is a powerful tool for our growth, healing, and expansion. It's a primary tool for a spiritual scientist. Keep in mind that backing up our intentions with demonstrated action is important. This is *practical spirituality*. Whether I am visualizing, chanting, or meditating, intention sets the course.

Invocation, such as prayer or calling in the Light, is a powerful and crucial aspect of engaging in a spiritual approach to healing. We invite the presence of *radiant energies* to work with us. An effective way to do this is as unconditionally as possible to allow the intelligence of Spirit to call the shots. We can always ask for specific things for the Highest Good.

Invocation

We use invocation because Universal Intelligence does not trespass into our goings-on without invitation. We create our own experiences, and invocation honors that. It also honors our request for the highest good. Here's a format I use as the basis for my invocation:

"Father, Mother God, I ask just now to be surrounded, protected, and filled with the Light of Loving. I ask that any karma, negativity, and imbalance be released, completed, and cleared through Grace. I ask that only that which is for the Highest Good of all concerned be allowed to come forward at this time. And I give my thanks."

I can pray specifically for myself, others, or any situation, place, or thing. Further, I always end the prayer by asking for the highest good for all concerned. Each of us can invite assistance and guidance in whatever way we like. It could be the higher light, Christ, Father-Mother God, Holy Spirit, Buddha, or whatever. Higher intelligence knows our intention. Our focus in prayer helps bring us into the Light and to bring Light into us.

Visualization

Visualization can be a powerful tool for healing. Be present and practice clarity when you visualize. The creative imagination is used in this and is a powerful tool to help manifest. Some spiritual practices use visualization as a way to practice opening the spiritual eyes. With clear intention over time, visualization can be training to begin to see clairvoyantly.

Olympic athletes use this method to train for exceptional physical mastery. They demonstrate the "taking action" part quite well with clear and persistent imaging.

That being said, visualization is not a daydream about what might be. It's seeing something taking place here and now. Being clear and focused is important so we don't pollute what we work to create. We achieve a great deal of healing and balance through clear intention and visualization.

There are a couple of visualization meditations I perform regularly as part of my normal daily self-care. One of them goes something like this:

I close my eyes and start with an invocation. Next, I visualize my energy body as an egg-shaped form of light comprised of white, gold, and other colors. I see my chakra centers as blobs of light or colored flowers with petals. I envision gold light coming from above my head down into my oval.

I take this to each chakra and envision healing, balancing, and vitalization. If I feel aches or pains in a specific area, I bring light to the area. If I have a certain issue, like anxiety or lack of purpose, I check in on that experience and then visualize light flowing into it. I visualize my physical body and bring light to each organ and each system. I may see certain colors or wait to see what light shows up. Some of them include sounds or chanting.

I sometimes use a pre-recorded, guided imagery mediation for visualization. Many spiritually oriented groups use guided meditations in their practices. Some have a number of them available. Explore and find what works for you.

Chanting

Chanting sacred tones is an ancient and powerful spiritual method. Word forms and sounds are energy frequencies. Each dimension we live in has sound frequencies present in those realms. Om or Aum are examples related to the mental realm. Chanting a sound of a specific dimension or realm brings alignment with its frequency. When we chant or sing various tones, aloud or inwardly, their energy frequencies begin to affect things. Be sure to apply an intention with this.

Some chants heal more than others. I have observed that, when I chant aloud, the actual vibration made by my vocal cords seems to affect my physical body more. When I chant inwardly, it may affect my ethereal bodies more. The only way I know what energy frequency a particular tone has is by direct experience. We can read about tones or words to chant, yet we must check it out in our own experience.

Most spiritual traditions have toning, chanting, or singing as part of their approach. In Christianity, hallelujah is enormously powerful. Aum does the same in Buddhism, and there are many in Hinduism.

Most shamanistic and native traditions include toning and chanting of sounds in their religions. A Native American medicine woman taught me the sound AHH. As we chanted it, my heart center began to open. This adds another dimension to rituals using chanting and singing.

The mental dimension is the source of Universal Mind, a repository of information. Emanating from the mental realm is a sound we know as OM or AUM which attunes us to this location and supports access to the information here. The OOOO in OM attunes to a higher frequency. The MMMM in OM grounds this frequency into the mental realm.

A teacher who spiritually travels the inner realms can add special significance to chanting tones. They can charge a tone with a specific energy for an individual or group with a specific purpose. A teacher may charge tones with either magnetic or spiritual energy frequencies. The highest good is integral to the charge, so they lift, complete, move, balance, clear, and transform as is appropriate with *radiant energies.*

The most powerful tone I came across is the HU, pronounced like the name Hugh, which is an ancient name for God. It contains intense energy frequencies transcending the magnetic realms. HU contains all other sounds within it. I find chanting it heals at all levels, especially helpful to a damaged human energy field. An alternative, ANIHU, adds empathy. It's excellent for groups to unify their consciousness.

When I chant words for their meanings, they begin to manifest the meaning. For example, the word God is a language symbol expressing the concept of Higher Power. As a symbol, sound vibrations have no relationship to what God is. Still, for me, if I chant God, my awareness opens to an experience of Higher Power.

I chant, "Healing my bodies" on my breath to direct the spiritual force to facilitate healing. I can chant "loving in," on my in-breath and "imbalances out" on the out-breath.

In ancient languages, the sound tones of a word closely matched the energy frequencies of whatever the word stood for. Experiment, and be careful not to overdo it. Be accountable for your own experience. These tones may be chanted inwardly, out loud, or in synchronization with the breath. Pay attention when using tones, and closely observe the results.

Meditation

Meditation in its original application simply described the practice of closing our eyes, going inside, and opening our awareness to our Authentic Self as a practice. This involves leaving awareness of the physical world and going into inner worlds. It is a practice of moving the center point of awareness to the Authentic Self, to become Soul-centered in awareness.

Newtonian science's need to prove something scientifically has turned the focus toward finding a demonstrated result. So many of us think about meditation in terms of what positive physical effects we can achieve. That's fine, as there are demonstrable physical results either way. Regardless of the perspective, meditation returns a value on many levels.

Closing our eyes, getting quiet, and going inside with our awareness is a great setup to facilitate healing and balancing. This type of meditation is a passive approach. Focusing on the breath and quieting the mind sets the stage for our inner *radiant energies* to begin aligning and healing. Again, the intention we sit down with is as critical as our invocation.

The mind cannot be stopped, even when we sleep. We just go mostly unconscious from it. The goal is to slow the mind down to minimal activity and then observe what takes place. Keep coming back to neutral observation. Focusing on the breath is an effective way to quiet the mind. The passive approach is to observe what appears as the consciousness quiets down. When the shopping list and work activities appear as thoughts, simply observe and refocus.

There are more active approaches to meditation. Closing the eyes, going in, and visualizing are also considered meditation. That is a more active approach. Saying a word mentally with each breath is an approach. For instance, inhaling equals love and exhaling equals peace.

The spiritual practice I follow is ancient. In Shabd Yoga or Soul Transcendence, the spiritual teacher charges specific tones with spiritual energy unique to the individual. There is a series of initiations that usually take years to receive. Each initiation has a tone and a level. These charged tones are energy frequency keys promoting transformation in consciousness and allowing access through invisible realms by connecting to the Sound Current.

Sound Current initiates sit for anywhere from twenty minutes to two hours a day, go inside, chant tones, and travel. Here in the West, because this is a very active meditative practice, we call it Spiritual Exercise.

We exercise the spiritual part of us. We give the mind something to do – chant the tones and practice allowing ourselves to follow the spiritual frequencies. In this practice, the initiate progresses through the magnetic realms, finally entering the spiritual realms.

The charged tones specifically engage higher-frequency *spiritual radiant energies* knowing how to, specifically for each person, heal, clear, balance, transform, and elevate our consciousness on all levels. It's a spiritually guided, conscious, active practice of evolvement into Soul-centered awareness. Ego-work unfolds naturally as part of the practice.

As our awareness moves into these higher spiritual frequencies, they naturally adjust, align, and balance our bodies, including the physical body, so we *sustain* Soul-centered awareness. The higher-frequency spiritual energies or *radiant energies* are the ones performing "miracles." Of course, they also utilize and activate magnetic energy frequencies since our physical, astral, causal, mental, and etheric bodies are magnetic frequencies.

When we invite and engage *radiant energies* through spiritual practices or methods, we receive tremendous real and concrete value. The founders of Alcoholics Anonymous were aware of the importance of *radiant energies* (they call it Higher Power) for healing as an integral part of the recovery program. This is not about belief. This is about the very real presence and activity of *radiant energies* precipitating out of the Universal Noetic Field.

Meditation as a practice of deeply connecting with our original spiritual essence is a powerful way to facilitate healing. Anytime we invite and engage the higher frequencies of *radiant energy*, the greater healing, balancing, and vitalizing effects we get throughout our whole consciousness.

Chapter 20:
Afterthoughts

"If you use drugs to experience higher levels of consciousness than what everyday life seems to offer, there are other methods that can give you more lasting and uplifting results…. Although the power of drugs is significant, once you activate your higher nature, the thrills that they offer pale in comparison. If you are looking for adventure, then discovering, exploring, and becoming more aware of who you truly are can be one of the greatest experiences of your life."

John-Roger DSS, *Spiritual High*

This chapter is a series of vignettes of afterthoughts. My spiritual teacher said that any words he used to try to explain the Divine, Original Universal Intelligence, or the Beloved were all lies. Words never adequately describe what spirituality actually is. I find this to be so true. Still, we do our best. I am inspired by poetry and writing, and in my own writing hope to pass along some inspiration.

Individual Growth and Preparation

This book so lightly skims across the surface of many things. The psychedelic experience is not a clear-cut something. I can't define it a certain way and have it be true across the board. In truth, each person has their own specific movement and experience in life. Each of us has a specific evolution. The timespan may be millions and sometimes billions of years. As Souls, holographic particles of the One, our process of experience and learning spans hundreds, thousands, or even millions of "lifetimes."

Each psychedelic experience is wholly guided by where we are in our evolutionary journey. This is very specific. What does Universal Intelligence allow us to experience, our Highest Good? What is the next step on our path of awakening? What was our life path intention for this lifetime?

When I was doing my high-dose trips I entered into profoundly deep mystical, spiritual experiences immediately and repeatedly. Those who tripped with me, not so much. Some of them never did have an experience like that. Some had only bad trips. Some had only recreational experiences.

Using psychedelics as entheogens, as a way to access altered states of consciousness gifts with profound and uplifting realizations, is a crap shoot. For some yes, for some no. Can we control the outcome? Based on my experience, and reading accounts by various psychedelic explorers, no, it doesn't work that way. It won't work because we each have our own specific pace in our evolution of consciousness. Each highest good is different.

This is a life-truth. Psychedelics or not, this is true. Life is just set up that way. But it also means that, for some, psychedelics provide access to truly high states of awareness. It gives them the profound and truthful experiences any spiritual path could give. They go to very high realms. They are taught by high beings in high realms.

This book is about the energetic human being and an energetic perspective on psychedelic use. The conditions, dynamics, and results of psychotropic use I describe are discoveries I made. They are discoveries and perceptions a group of energy medicine practitioners found by direct perception. They are conditions my spiritual teacher easily, normally, and directly perceived.

While there are no clear-cut absolute truths about any of it, to a large degree, the energetic findings I have shared take place. The information applies most of the time but not all the time. This is true for everything in the world. I handle this by taking on the mantle of a spiritual scientist. I check it out by direct experience to see what works or doesn't work for me.

Beyond Mind

I was probably around 30 when I became aware, by direct experience, that who I am in essence transcends the mind. During this time, I found my mind to be a distraction, it just seemed to get in the way most of the time. I noticed it never shut up. I noticed it went in all sorts of directions and off on all kinds of tracks. I found it was a non-stop engine of thoughts and even ran all night as I slept.

When I sat down to do my spiritual exercises, it seemed to be the primary source for any and all distractions sidetracking or blocking me from getting into higher, deeper states of consciousness. Please shut up!

My spiritual teacher taught something he called mental dominion. To be successful at mental dominion would mean that, while I couldn't stop my mind, I could learn to watch it do its thing while I lifted above it, left it, and traveled into higher spiritual states unimpeded by it.

In my mid-fifties, I finally succeeded at mental dominion. During that time, my consciousness moved its central anchor point from ego to Soul. My reality shifted entirely, and the place I lived my life from changed. My mind still did its thing but no longer ran the show. Now I could move past my mind relatively easily. I was never all that interested in information levels, I wanted a direct experience. Now information levels were like eating cardboard. It has substance but is tasteless and uninteresting.

Sustainability

When I was first seeking direct experiences of mystical, spiritual transcendence, the sustainability of experiences didn't cross my mind. As I dove into high-dose psychedelic use, the depth and profundity of the experiences were enough. Then, like many psychedelic explorers before me, I came to the after-experience. I missed the direct ongoing experience of the psychedelic high.

Fortunately, I didn't have to go to the depth of longing that many experience. I didn't have to enter the experience of post-bliss, post-transcendence depression. I didn't have to go there because I moved right into a relationship with a rare and true spiritual master who walked the talk and delivered on the spiritual experiences he taught.

Soon after meeting my teacher, I began having direct experiences again of those highly mystical states. During the first few years working with him, I began to ponder the reality of sustainability or not. There was a principal value of the spiritual teaching and practice I was learning. The experience of expanding spiritual awareness and transformation taking place sustained me.

I talk about "effective" spiritual practice. From the beginning of my quest, I sought direct experience, not just information. Sure, I love how satisfying it is to intellectually explore ideas or a particular subject, but direct experience is the golden treasure. I learned, as a spiritual scientist, to practice methods to discover, by direct experience, whether they work or not for me. A spiritual scientist cuts through the red tape of the mind to find what produces the sought-after experience.

So, I found a spiritual practice that brought Spontaneous Transcendence. Doing this practice, I discovered that spiritual awareness has no endpoint, it's always expanding. I discovered there are many levels of self-realization and God-consciousness. The samadhi or nirvana I originally sought was simply a stepping stone. A primary quality of the living Spirit is infinite movement. To say that is paradoxical. In the presence of Absolute Stillness and Nothingness is infinite movement.

I also discovered something I didn't much like when I realized it. This discovery has a set of parameters. These parameters relate to our humanness. A principal purpose of life is to have experience. Somehow the Beloved, who is fully complete, is in a constant state of expansion. We are the living instruments of this expansion. Our expansion is the Beloved expanding.

The limitations of human experience are purposeful. My spiritual teacher would sit his body down, go inside, and Soul travel. He could see and know exactly where and what anyone he focused on was doing, thinking, and wearing no matter where they were. He traveled all the magnetic dimensions of the Web of Life – astral, causal, mental, etheric – and brought back conscious awareness and remembrance of his travels. He was wholly Soul aware and traveled the singular energy dimensions above Soul. He taught by demonstration.

I learned that, while I may travel consciously in multiple dimensions simultaneously, and while I may enter states of spiritual awareness that access the wisdom pools and tap into bliss and ecstasy, as long as I am human, I cannot sustain this. I am very human today with all my mental gyrations, emotional waves, and day-to-day tasks. Tomorrow, another transcendent experience presents itself, and my realizations of the revelations of life expand.

I have intense Spontaneous Transcendental experiences that are just as intense as drug-induced transcendental experiences. I am aware of the purposefulness of these experiences. I encounter high-frequency spiritual energy downloading into my bodies. I see my nervous system light up. I am aware the Light knows just how much I can take. Each time this happens my physical ability to withstand and hold the energy expands.

Still, these experiences have clear beginnings and ends to them. Their intensity is not sustainable. During these downloads, some amount of wisdom inherently present in the *radiant energies* comes into conscious awareness. It's direct seeing into the mysterious workings within the living intelligence of Universal Noetic Field. Some amount of wisdom is brought to conscious awareness.

The wisdom sustains. The frequency adjustment to my bodies sustain. Sometimes there are health benefits that sustain.

My personal movement from ego-centered to Soul-centered expands into greater Soul awareness. Natural inherent qualities in Spirit or Soul are humanly expressed as peace, joy, enthusiasm, and loving. For me, as time went by, I found myself in the presence of loving more and more.

The loving I speak of is a way to describe the Being field of the Beloved. It's the place where the very fabric of creation, the fabric of self, is made of loving. Experience of this may be profoundly neutral, an experience of pure unadulterated, unconditioned living energy. Or it may contain the nuances of acceptance, mercy, caring, gentleness, and unconditional forgiveness, along with aspects of the wisdom of the Beloved.

While the intensity of the transcendental experience is not sustainable, nor was it ever meant to be, I dare say we all want sustainable fulfillment. Fulfillment for each of us is very individual. It depends a great deal on where we are in the evolutionary journey of our Soul.

As a spiritual scientist, I decide what fulfillment means to me. Then I set out to discover, by direct experience, what I can do to manifest the experience of fulfillment. I seek ways and means to bring fulfillment that is sustainable.

The Grace Field

One of the great mysteries of life is how we all walk a path of awakening, but any path is an illusion. For those of us who are seekers, we see ourselves on a path or journey moving toward some sort of destination. We seek transcendence, or samadhi, or the place where we come to a realization of who we truly are, and how life truly works. We seek mystical experience and spiritual enlightenment. We seek all that we already are.

If we do our work, if the Beloved has mercy, and if it is our time, we pass beyond the state of separate consciousness and become the Beloved. One of my names for this is the Grace Field. How is it that, not only, am I all I have sought but have always been so? I have lived in the Grace Field eternally. There is no path or journey. What a beautiful illusion the Beloved has created.

In the experience of the Grace Field is the One beingness of all things. In the beingness of the Beloved is an incomprehensible loving. Here is the field beyond right doing and wrong doing, for the field and all in the field are made of the same substance, love. There is no ability to see the negative and positive. What is seen is not the sides of the coin, but the coin itself. The One coin has a head on one side and a tail on the other. Either side is the same.

There is great beauty in the way each face is different. There is delight that there is both an oak tree and a willow. The huge variety in the appearance of form is a blessing. All experience is a blessing, the way each of our senses – taste, touch, seeing, hearing, and feeling – allow experiences of the Beloved. Our heartbeat pumping blood through our veins is a gift. The bellow of our lungs is a gift.

In the Grace Field all awareness, all that is present, all that comes and goes, and all the activities on all levels are a gift of the Beloved. All form is an aspect of the Beloved. The blue sky, floating clouds, and wind rustling the leaves of the trees speak the wisdom of ages. Within the darkness of the night is an illuminating light. Welcome to illumination. Rejoice in living love. Walk now in the consciousness of the One.

Sound Current

I am an initiate in the Sound Current tradition. It's a rigorous approach, much more so in countries like India. Initiates in Far Eastern traditions follow cultural guidelines as well as the core spiritual practice. Guidelines such as what they eat or drink, how they dress, or their marital life. My spiritual teacher stripped away the cultural trappings and taught the bare-bones methodology.

Still, the Sound Current path is very narrow. Narrow is the way. Soon it's like threading a needle. So much baggage must be released. An essential part of the initiatory process requires the *ability* to hold and sustain high-frequency spiritual energies on all levels. The initiation process is sequential, based on demonstrable experience and ability. The process takes time.

We move as a movement of spiritual inner awareness through each magnetic realm (physical, astral, causal, mental, and etheric.) We clear karma, enough to passage through and stabilize our consciousness on that level. I spent about two years in the astral, then around three years in the causal, and three in the mental. Then I spent eight years in the etheric before being able to handle, in a minimal way, entrance to the Soul realm. This is an incredibly fast passage, relatively.

We expand and grow enough in consciousness to proceed to the next level. Soul Transcendence is wholly ability based. Conjecture or belief won't do it. The writing on the wall is clearly seen. As we self-realize, we remember ourselves back into our original essential selves, Authentic Selves, or Soul. We are this already. Our accrual of cause and effect over millennia brings wisdom but also becomes a conditioned blockage to our remembrance.

Sound Current spiritual practice is very specific. It's of the highest order requiring diligent commitment. It's not for everyone. For me, I needed direct experience of all the mysteries of life. I was done with any possible mental pursuit of knowledge. It takes dedication to walk the path and takes even greater dedication to hold consciousness as we progress. This path requires a guide to show the way. A teacher who has the full ability to see, know, and travel the way is such a spiritual teacher.

So, for me, while psychedelic drugs were part of my journey to direct experience, if I were to indulge that approach now, it would disconnect me from sustaining higher consciousness. As we achieve higher states and can sustain them, psychotropic effects become lower experiences. If I compare the euphoria of Spontaneous Transcendence with the euphoria of marijuana, there is no comparison. A marijuana high is profoundly lesser and lower.

If I used marijuana now, the high would be a haze or fog blocking me from actual high states of awareness. If I were to use a psychedelic now, the neuro-biochemical effect would likely interrupt my state of stabilized spiritual consciousness. If I went back to repeated use of a psychotropic it would certainly disconnect me spiritually.

Yes, Sound Current initiation is very specific. It is a proven path, a shortcut, to extremely high levels of transcendence and sustainable spiritual awareness. If I have achieved sustainable spiritual awareness, then I did it over time using a spiritual practice that works. And once, having entered these sustainable states of wisdom and loving, if I were to revert to psychedelic use, it would take me backward.

Our beliefs and ideas about all this don't change what actually takes place. Psychotropics stop short of sustainable spiritual awareness. They not only stop short but also, in the end, block us from sustainable transcendence and spiritual awareness.

GLOSSARY

Here are the meanings for terms in the book as I define them.

Allopathic Medicine: Modern or Western Medicine. Treatment of illness or disease by treating the presenting symptom.

Authentic Self: A spiritual psychology word for Soul. Our original essential self, the original energy powering each consciousness. Our true self beyond ego.

Awareness: The basis of consciousness, an essential quality of consciousness, constant of consciousness, the primary quality of Soul.

Consciousness Teacher: A person that supports us in our "ego-work" and provides training, ceremony, or ritual to initiate and support our growth and evolution.

Curriculum of the Soul: As spiritual beings, with purposeful, intelligent guidance from Source, we create the curriculum of our Life Path. This curriculum includes opportunities to complete past actions (karma) and opportunities for experience to increase wisdom and further our evolution.

Energetic Construct or Structure: A psycho-dynamic energetic form in the human energy field acting as a holographic particle containing a thought, belief, or judgment held in relation to a previous experience.

Entheogen: A chemical substance or drug, often of plant origin, which is ingested to produce altered states of consciousness for religious or spiritual purposes.

Heuristic: Learning by self-discovery through experience rather than an academic study of something outside of oneself. The applied method of experiential learning within oneself.

Individual Noetic Field: Our energetic anatomy. Our energetic nature is an aspect of Universal Intelligence, also the aura.

Lens of Perception: The filter through which we perceive the world and ourselves, formed by gender identity, cultural education, experience, what we are taught by parents, peers, and in school, religious belief, political belief, and all beliefs.

Life Path: A plan created by Soul and Universal Intelligence that all Souls embody with, outlining the plan for a lifetime. As a plan, it has wide parameters giving individual consciousness the responsibility of directing and fulfilling it. A plan to support the evolution of the individual Soul.

Newtonian Lens of Perception: A linear and mechanistic way of seeing. The Universe is "like-a-machine" with interlocking parts, each part is observed and studied separately.

Noetic: Derived from the Greek word *nous*, referring to the advent of intellect or the presence of an intelligent purposive principle. Noetic ascribes intelligence and awareness to the infinite Web of Life.

Noetic Balancing: Approaches psychological healing and balancing through human energy anatomy. Psychological states or issues are expressions of energy body conditions or states. Blocks, imbalances, and issues are accessed through Energetic Constructs present in the aura to be released or balanced. In a Noetic Balancing session, the balancee lies on a massage table fully clothed, and the balancer, using a pendulum to increase sensitivity and connection, opens the energy field of the client and balances on the physical level, emotional level, and mental/spiritual levels. The practitioner facilitates healing in conscious cooperation with Universal Intelligence, *radiant energies,* and the Highest Good. Healing is self-empowerment-based.

Noetic Field Therapy (NFT): A results-based, practical system of healing founded on ancient mystical healing knowledge coupled with modern Spiritual Psychology and Quantum physics. See Noetic Balancing.

Noetic Field or Web: A concept that describes the interconnectedness of all things. All life is one web of being, and the web itself is inherently intelligent.

Pharmacological Approach: Application of chemical substances or drugs to the physical body to treat imbalance, illness, or disease.

Psychotropic: A chemical substance or drug that directly affects emotional or mental experience, not just physical biology.

Psychotropic Transcendence: A psychotropic drug such as LSD is introduced into the human body prompting biochemical cascades primarily in the brain and neural network mimicking Spontaneous Transcendence. See Spontaneous Transcendence.

Psychedelic: "Mind-manifesting." The word has been used more as a colloquial expression to describe intensely alternate/expansive consciousness-altering drug experiences.

Psychoactive: See Psychotropic.

Quantum Theory of Physics: A scientific discipline that explores the foundations and attributes of matter and describes the nature of matter as energy. All energy comes in discrete bundles, called quanta, consisting of waves (rate of vibration-frequency).

Quantum Lens of Perception: The *lens of perception* that sees all matter and human consciousness as energy frequencies, including our physical body. All energy bodies that make up our "spiritual" energetic anatomy are energy frequencies. Therefore, our consciousness is a "quanta" of various energy frequencies that coalesce to form what we experience and know as human consciousness.

Radiant Energy: In my definition, *radiant energy* is an energy form beyond dual, bipolar electromagnetic. It is a singular energy form. Magnetic energy has a positive pole and a negative pole. In physics, radiant energy is energy in its waveform, thus making it electromagnetic energy.

Spiritual Psychology: Spiritual Psychology recognizes the Authentic Self. Humans are recognized as spiritual/energetic beings. Education under Spiritual Psychology is experiential and transformational. Approaches to healing and balancing the ego structure are based on transformation rather than on treating symptoms. The approach is to heal ego structures by awakening to our Authentic Selves.

Spiritual Science: Utilizing the methodology of physical science: ask a question, create a hypothesis, design an experiment, do the experiment and collect data, draw conclusions. To study oneself rather than to study things in the world outside oneself. Inherently heuristic.

Spiritual Scientist: One who uses a scientific method on him/herself to expand awareness of their true original nature as a spiritual being.

Spontaneous Transcendence: Transcendence that is naturally occurring in the course of one's life and is not substance-induced. It may take place through spiritual methodologies such as prayer or meditation. Spontaneous Transcendence is the result of the presence of *radiant energies.*

Practical Spirituality: A practice of spiritual methods for consciousness expansion and spiritual awakening that is workable in normal, everyday life. It recognizes that normal, everyday life is inherently designed for expansion and awakening.

Spiritual Teacher: A master teacher who demonstrates the primary qualities of Spirit – joy, enthusiasm, and unconditional Loving. An individual who teaches from direct experience and self-gathered wisdom, rather than from mental knowledge or memory. They deliver direct experience to the student. Their teaching transcends time and space. They actively work with students in the dream or sleep state to facilitate *radiant energies* and transmit keys to access spiritual consciousness and realms.

Shabd Yoga, Sound Current Teaching: Attunement to the Sound Current as a rigorous spiritual methodology, guided by a living teacher wherein a student is given spiritually charged tones to chant. Chanting tones activate transformation and awaken the student spiritually. It is an ancient approach involving direct transmission of *radiant energies* from teacher to student leading to Soul-Centered awareness. Generally, a lifelong practice.

Sound Current: Sound precedes Light and is the original spiritual essence emanating from the original Source. All creations, universes, and worlds are formed by the purposeful emanation of Sound from the Creator. The Sound Current is the shortcut super highway to ultimate self-realization by conscious attunement. All dimensions and forms have Sound as their ultimate substance. It is perceived in many ways, such as unconditional loving or the Beloved.

Soul Transcendence: The spiritual practice to awaken awareness at the Soul level, above the psychic/material worlds first, then awakening awareness into the high spiritual realms above Soul. To achieve the highest ultimate experience of self-realization. Called Shabd Yoga in Eastern spiritual traditions.

Transcendence: A direct experience of the intelligent Web of Life with mystical and spiritual realizations.

Transformation: A change that stays changed.

Universal Noetic Field: A Noetic Field Therapy term ascribing intelligence to the Web of Life, God, or the infinite Energy Field of Spirit.

Zero Point Field: A physics term describing the energy of the vacuum. It is the ground state of all fields or the constant source state for all things that are always present. It is the starting point for all fields and the energy constant. Western Science's concept of an infinite original Energy Field of Spirit or Source.

BIBLIOGRAPHY

American Psychiatric Association, *DSM-IV-TR: Diagnostic and Statistical Manual of Mental Disorders,* 4th ed, 2000.

Bache, Christopher M. *LSD and the Mind of the Universe: Diamonds From Heaven*, 2019.

Brennan, Barbara Ann, *Hands of Light*, 1987.

Blake, William. *The Complete Poetry and Prose of William Blake*, edited by David Erdman, 1982.

Bohm, David. *Science, Order, and Creativity: A Dramatic New Look at the Creative Roots of Science and Life.* NY, NY: Bantam Book, 1987.

Brown, David Jay. *Psychedelic Drug Research: A Comprehensive Review*, 2012.

Brown, David Jay. *Frontiers of Psychedelic Consciousness*, 2015.

Bruyere, Rosalyn L. *Wheels of Light: Chakras, Auras, and the Healing Energy of the Body*, 1994.

"Cannabis Use Is Quantitatively Associated with Nucleus Accumbens and Amygdala Abnormalities in Young Adult Recreational Users" *Journal of Neuroscience*, vol. 34, no. 16, 2014, pp. 5529-5538, doi: 10.1523/JNEUROSCI.4745-13.2014.

Capra, Fritjof. *The Web of Life,* 1996.

Castaneda, Carlos. *The Teachings of Don Juan: A Yaqui Way of Knowledge*, 1968.

Chopra, Deepak. *Perfect Health*, 1991.

Craighead, Edward W., et al. *Psychopathology: History, Diagnosis, and Empirical Foundations*, 2008.

Deikman, Arthur, et al. *Alternate States of Consciousness; Multiple Perspectives on the Study of Consciousness*, edited by Norman E. Zinberg, 1979.

Doblin, Rick, et al. *Manifesting Minds, an anthology from MAPS, A Review of Psychedelics in Science, Medicine, Sex, and Spirituality*, 2014.

Eden, Donna and Feinstein, David. *Energy Medicine*, 1998.

Farrell, Ted and Mackenzie, Lorrie. *Learning to Swim in the Quantum Soup*, 1998.

Gerber M.D., Richard. *Vibrational Medicine*, 2001.

Goldsmith, Neal M. *Psychedelic Healing: The Promise of Entheogens for Psychotherapy and Spiritual Development*, 2011.

Hawkins, David R. *Power vs Force: The Hidden Determinants of Human Behavior*, 1998.

Hay, Louise L. *You Can Heal Your Life*, 2004.

Hulnick Ph.D., Ronald H. and Hulnick Ph.D.., Mary R. *Loyalty to Your Soul: The Heart of Spiritual Psychology*, 2010.

Hulnick Ph.D., Ronald H. and Hulnick Ph.D.., Mary R. *Remembering the Light Within A Course in Soul-Centered Living*, 2017.

Huxley, Aldous. *The Divine Within*, 1992.

Huxley, Aldous. *The Doors of Perception*, 2009.

Huxley, Aldous. *The Perennial Philosophy*, 2009.

Johnson, Julian P. *The Path Of the Masters: The Science of Surat Shabd Yoga*, 1972.

John-Roger. *Fulfilling Your Spiritual Promise*, 2006.

John-Roger. *Loving Each Day*, Movement of Spiritual Inner Awareness, msia.org, 2023.

John-Roger. *Passage into Spirit*, 2005.

John-Roger. *Psychic Protection*, 1997.

John-Roger, *Spiritual High: Alternatives to Drugs and Substance Abuse*, 2005.

John-Roger, *Spiritual Warrior*, 1998.

Kilham, Chris. *The Ayahuasca Test Pilots Handbook: The Essential Guide to Ayahuasca Journeying*, 2014.

Kowl, A., et al. *High Times Encyclopedia of Recreational Drugs*, 1978.

Leary, Timothy, et al. *The Psychedelic Experience*, 2007.

Lipton, Bruce H. *The Biology of Belief*, 2008.

McTaggart, Lynne. *The Field*, 2002.

McTaggart, Lynne. *The Intention Experiment*, 2007.

Morton, John. *Loving Each Day*. Movement of Spiritual Inner Awareness, msia.org, 2023.

Myss, Caroline. *Anatomy of the Spirit*, 1996.

Myss, Caroline and Shealy, Norman C. *The Creation of Health*, 1993.

Power, Ellavivian. *The Auric Mirror*, 1968.

Radin, Dean. *Entangled Minds: Extrasensory Experiences in a Quantum Reality*, 2006.

Ram Dass and Alpert, Richard. *Be Here Now*, 1971.

Rich, Mark. *Energetic Anatomy*, 2004.

Richards, William A. *Sacred Knowledge; Psychedelics and Religious Experiences*, 2015.

Schwarz, Jack. *Human Energy Systems*, 1980.

Stafford, Peter. *Psychedelics Encyclopedia*, 1977.

Strassman M.D., Rick. *DMT: The Spirit Molecule: A Doctor's Revolutionary Research into the Biology of Near-Death and Mystical Experiences*, 2001.

Stevens, Jay. *Storming Heaven: LSD and the American Dream*, 1987.

Sudman, Natalie. *Application of Impossible Things: My Near-Death Experience in Iraq*, 2014.

Sui, Choa Kok. *Advanced Pranic Healing*, 1992.

Sui, Choa Kok. *Pranic Healing*, 1990.

Sui, Choa Kok. *The Ancient Science & Art of Pranic Psychotherapy*, 1989.

Tart, Charles T. *Altered States of Consciousness*, 1990.

Tart, Charles T. *States of Consciousness*, 1975.

Tolle, Eckhart. *The Power of Now*, 1999.

Waterman EdD, Robert D. *Eyes Made of Soul: The Theory and Practice of Noetic Balancing*, 2010.

Waterman EdD, Robert D. *Foot Prints of Eternity: Ancient Wisdom Applied to Modern Psychology*, 2006.

Waterman EdD, Robert D. *Mystery of the Square and Circle: A Guide to Spiritual Discovery Based on Ageless Wisdom*, 1995.

Waterman EdD., Robert D. *Self-Forgiveness: An Act of Life*, 1976.

Waterman EdD., Robert D. *The Human Energy Fields: Guidelines for Transformational Counseling*, 1981.

Waterman EdD., Robert D. *Transcendental Leadership: We Bring Love*, 2021.

Waterman EdD, Robert D and Thorne M.A. Karey C. *Power of Love: Ways and Means*, 2019.

Wilber, Ken, *Integral Spirituality*, 2007.

Yogananda, Paramahansa. *Autobiography of a Yogi*, 2006.

About Winston Hampton

Winston Hampton has been an avid spiritual seeker since his early teens. At 13, he felt driven to discover the meaning of life. His drug days as a teen became a psychedelic exploration into mystical realms. He became a high-dose psychedelic trip guide at 17. He read the Bible, the Bhagavad Gita, and any spiritual scripture he could find, intent on finding a spiritual path that would deliver a sustainable transcendent experience. Influenced by beatniks and hippies he began writing poetry and stream of consciousness as a teen.

He worked in restaurants, on a tugboat barge as a deckhand, and served on a Mississippi River paddleboat. He was a drug dealer. He hitchhiked back and forth across the country several times, once as a disillusioned member leaving the Hare Krishna movement. He took up farming and motorcycling. He lived in Tokyo for a year to start college.

At age 23, he left the world of drugs and met outstanding consciousness teachers. He met his spiritual teacher in a dream and soon after met him physically and began a lifelong spiritual practice of Soul Transcendence. Over the next 10 years, he immersed himself in self-growth, ego-work, and energy medicine training.

In married life, he helped raise four kids and dabbled in several careers. He became a house designer and builder, a cabinet maker, and a master woodworker. He loves writing and reading poetry because he experiences it as an altered state beyond the mind. He hopes to write about his experiences as a spiritual scientist practicing practical spirituality in ways that could be inspiring to others.

Winston currently lives in Bozeman, Montana with his wife, who is also ruthless about spiritual awakening. They love to hike, snowshoe, cross-country ski, camp, and go fly-fishing. Winston regularly visits his kids who are now making babies. As well as his regular out-of-doors activities, he spends time writing, feeding the dogs, renovating the house, creating a food forest, meditating, and doing online Zoom workshops and events related to awakening spiritually.

Made in the USA
Monee, IL
21 November 2023